PREFACE.

In first introducing to the public the "Unicode," by means of "The Universal Telegraphic Phrase-Book," * it is well to give a few preliminary explanations and directions.

All the great submarine Telegraph Companies, and almost all foreign countries and colonies, have adopted the word-tariff, or system of charging a certain sum for each word, and Great Britain has practically done so. by the changes effected during the last Parliament. Every person who has heretofore sent telegraphic messages abroad has learned by experience the economy of condensation, and the advantage of the use of a Code known to both sender and receiver. By this means the substance of a message embracing a dozen ordinary words may be conveyed in a single code-word, with a fulness and clearness not to be otherwise attained unless at a prohibitive cost. The same effect is discovered in inland telegraphic communication under the new arrangements. The sixpenny telegram is found, except under special circumstances, to be a misnomer, the unavoidable length of the addresses (where the expense of registering a cypher has not been incurred by the Receiver), and the name of the Sender and Receiver absorbing so many of the twelve words as frequently to leave only two or three available for the text of the telegram. Attention is therefore naturally turned to condensation, and, as a necessary consequence, to coding.

The Code-Book hitherto has been distinguished by two features —a high price and an attempted exclusiveness. The "Unicode" aims at precisely opposite qualities, viz., a low price and a universality of employment, so that not only in all offices, but in clubs, hotels, and private residences copies shall be found and freely used.

* A Pocket Edition of this book, of convenient size, is also published, price 2s. 6d.

An example will best demonstrate the mode of using, and the economy effected. Say the following is the message in full:—

TO	Smith, 100, Prince Rupert Road, Shepherd's Bush.			
Jones	dines	with	us	this
evening	and	remains	the	night
				Smith

Here the address and signature take eight words, and the body of the message ten, making eighteen words in all, or six extra to pay for; whereas by using the "Unicode" the message is reduced to ten words, and runs thus :—

TO	Smith, 100, Prince Rupert Road, Shepherd's Bush.			
Jones	Coctivus			
	Smith			

But in foreign telegrams the difference is more striking. The rate, for instance, from South America is ten shillings per word, and the following message (without reckoning the address) would cost £3 :—"Order executed before your telegram arrived;" whereas the "Unicode" word "*Obumbro*" would convey the same message at a cost of ten shillings, or a saving of £2 10s.

Many phrases which at first sight would appear too unnecessarily minute, notably in domestic affairs, are purposely inserted as being those which experience shows are in actual daily use, notwithstanding their heavy cost for transmission.

Users of existing codes have constantly experienced difficulty and misunderstanding from the fact that, English words being used for the cyphers, the messages have at times read intelligibly in the ordinary and not the code meaning of the words, and the Receiver has not known which to adopt. This has been entirely obviated in the " Unicode " by exclusively employing for the cyphers Latin words which strictly conform to the regulations of the International Telegraph Conferences held at Paris, London, and Berlin. An equally important point has also been carefully borne in mind. It is generally known that the telegraphic alphabet is composed of three elements: the dot, the dash, and the space. These symbols may with great facility be transposed in transmission, causing words, however dissimilar in ordinary language (such as *fancy* and *pantry*) to be confounded one with another in the process of telegraphy. This compilation, however, has been made under the personal supervision of telegraphic experts of long experience, and it is claimed for it that the cypher words are from their telegraphic construction the least liable to erroneous transmission by the operators.

The cypher words have been arranged alphabetically, and the phrases are likewise so arranged, having regard to what is in each the principal or key-word.

Not the least valuable feature (and it is a novel one) in the present volume is the addition of a list of important firms and establishments in Great Britain, with their registered telegraphic addresses, who will receive telegrams in the " Unicode." This list will be hereafter increased, and for this purpose intimations are invited from those firms at home and abroad who desire their names to be added. These should be sent to the care of the Publishers, and addressed to the Editors of the " Unicode," who will be grateful for any suggestions for improvements and additions.

To allow for the composition of a small private code available only to the individual compilers, and not to be adopted hereafter in the " Unicode " for specific phrases for public use, a few pages with cypher words only have been added, to which phrases may be attached as desired.

NOTE TO SECOND EDITION.

The compilers refer to the following communication which they have received :—

"I have examined from the point of view of a telegraph operator of long standing, several Codes which have been recently published, and I emphatically pronounce the UNICODE to be the only one I have seen where the hand of the expert can be discovered. In one of the other compilations it is claimed as a merit that none of the cypher words exceed five letters. This, however, is a serious blot, and condemns the book in my judgment. In two Codes I observe a free use of manufactured words, and yet, for extra-European correspondence, such words can be and are generally rejected by the Cable Companies. Naturally it is preferable that the operator should transmit messages where the meaning is clear and the words as usual, but as it seems evident that the use of Codes will grow day by day it is to be hoped that the public will continue to employ one so workman-like and systematic as the UNICODE."

October, 1886.

POSSIBLE TRANSFORMATIONS OF TELEGRAPH SIGNALS.

LETTER.	MORSE SIGNAL.	POSSIBLE SUBSTITUTION.			
A	· —	ET			
B	— · · ·	TS	NI	DE	
C	— · — ·	NN	TR	TEN	KE
D	— · ·	TI	NE		
E	·				
F	· · — ·	IN	ER	UE	
G	— — ·	ME	TN		
H	· · · ·	SE	ES	II	
I	· ·	EE			
J	· — — —	EO	ATT	AM	WT
K	— · —	TA	NT	TT	
L	· — · ·	AI	RE	ED	
M	— —	TT			
N	— ·	TE			
O	— — —	TM	MT		
P	· — — ·	WE	AN	EG	EME
Q	— — · —	MA	GT	TK	
R	· — ·	AE	EN		
S	· · ·	IE	EI		
T	—				
U	· · —	EA	IT		
V	· · · —	ST	EU	IA	
W	· — —	EM	AT		
X	— · · —	NA	TU	DT	
Y	— · — —	NM	TW	KT	
Z	— — · ·	MI	GE	TD	

REGULÁTIONS AS TO TRANSMISSION OF TELEGRAMS.

THE rules and regulations which govern the telegraphic communication between various portions of the world are laid down by the International Telegraph Conferences which meet periodically in one or other of the capitals of Europe, and the following gives the effect of those which should be most widely known :—

All telegrams should be legibly written.

Telegrams may be composed of plain language, of code language, or of secret language.

Telegrams in plain language must present a clear meaning in any one of the languages admitted for telegraphic correspondence.

Telegrams in code language must consist of words not exceeding ten letters in length, each of them presenting a clear meaning, but not necessarily any consecutive sense, and belonging to any one or to all of the following languages, but to no other, viz. :—English, French, German, Italian, Dutch, Portuguese, Spanish, and Latin.

Code words containing more than ten letters are charged at cypher rate.

Proper names are not admitted in the text of code messages unless used in their natural sense.

The Company can demand the production of the codes and vocabularies, for the purpose of controlling the execution of the preceding regulations.

Private telegrams composed of secret letters such as a b x y z, are not admitted in extra-European correspondence.

Illegitimate combinations of words contrary to the usage of the language, and abbreviated and wrongly spelt words, are inadmissible.

The maximum length of a single word is fixed at 15 letters in European telegrams, and at 10 letters in extra-European telegrams, any additional letters being counted and charged for as extra words at the rate of 15 or 10 letters respectively to the word.

Any instruction the sender may have to give as to the delivery at destination, prepayment of reply, acknowledgment of receipt, to its being a collated telegram, &c., should be written immediately before the address. These indications may be given in the following abbreviated forms, when they will be counted as one word only :—

RP for Reply paid.	FS for To follow.
TC ,, Collation paid.	RPD ,, Urgent reply paid.
CR ,, Acknowledgment of receipt.	PR ,, Post registered.
PP ,, Postage paid.	EP ,, Estaffette paid.
XP ,, Express paid.	

Any sender may request by writing the instruction : "Télégramme à faire suivre" (*i.e.* to follow) or "(FS)" (which is charged for), immediately before the address, that the terminal office shall cause his telegram to follow the receiver within the limits of Europe.

The charge to the first address only is prepaid, the cost of further transmission being collected on delivery.

INDEX.

UNIVERSAL TELEGRAPHIC PHRASE-BOOK.

Abandon the negotiations . . . . Abactus

(Able)—Am *able* to . . . . . Abazea
    Am not *able* to . . . . . . Abdite
    Are you *able* to . . . . . Abdixi
    Have you been *able* to . . . . Abdo
    Shall be *able* to . . . . Abdomen
    Shall not be *able* to . . . . Abductus

Absence has prevented my earlier reply . Abequito
    Can do nothing during *absence* of — . . Abeuntis
    Can do nothing in your *absence* . . . Abfore

Accept. (Refer to DECLINE.)
    Cannot *accept* less than — . . . . Abhorreo
    Do not *accept* . . . . . . Abitio

Acceptance paid away, too late to stop . . Abjecte
    Acceptance paid into bank, cannot be withdrawn . . . . . . Abjectio
    Acceptance will be renewed . . . Abjicio
    Cannot renew *acceptance* . . . . Abjudico
    Have withdrawn *acceptance* . . . Abjuro
    Refuse to renew *acceptance* . . . Ablaqueo
    Will withdraw *acceptance* on receipt of bank order for — . . . . . . Ablego

Accident has occurred to train on the — . . Abludo

Met with an *accident*	Abnato
Met with an *accident,* cannot keep appointment	Abnepos
Met with an *accident,* come as quickly as you can	Abneptis
Met with an *accident,* must postpone visit .	Abnodo
Met with an *accident,* must remain here, letter by post	Abnormis
Met with an *accident,* not very serious .	Abolesco
Met with an *accident,* only slight . .	Abolevi
Met with an *accident,* very serious . .	Abolitio
Met with an *accident,* which prevents my leaving	Abominor
Met with an *accident,* will return . .	Aborior
Met with an *accident,* boat upset, all safe .	Abrasi
Met with an *accident,* boat upset, remain here till you come	Abreptus
Met with an *accident,* boat upset, send a change here	Abrogo
Met with an *accident,* carriage upset, not hurt	Abrumpo
Met with an *accident,* carriage upset, slightly hurt	Abruptio
Met with an *accident,* collision, not hurt .	Abscedo
Met with an *accident,* collision, seriously hurt	Abscindo
Met with an *accident,* collision, slightly hurt	Abscisse
Met with an *accident,* come . . .	Absens
Met with an *accident,* but need not come .	Absentia
What is the nature of the *accident* . .	Absilio
When did the *accident* occur . . .	Absolvo
Where did the *accident* occur . . .	Absonus

Account. (Refer to Place.)

Account is being made out . . .	Absorbeo
Account is forwarded to-day . . .	Abstineo

Account is overdrawn	Abstraxi
Not on my *account*	Abstrudo
Not on our *account*	Absurdus
Not on your *account*	Abundo
Placed to your *account* the sum of — . .	Abusque

Acknowledge.   (Refer to Documents, Letter, Remittance, Telegram.)

Acknowledge by telegram receipt of documents	Abutor
Acknowledge by telegram receipt of letter .	Acacia
Acknowledge by telegram receipt of remittance	Academia
Why have you not *acknowledged* receipt of documents	Acapna
Why have you not *acknowledged* receipt of letter	Acapnon
Why have you not *acknowledged* receipt of remittance	Acatium
Why have you not *acknowledged* receipt of telegram	Accanto

Act as for yourself . . . . . .

Act as for yourself	Accedo
Act as you think best	Accelero
Act on my letter	Acceptio
Act on my previous telegram . . .	Acceptus
Act on my previous instructions . . .	Accerso
— is empowered to *act* on my (or our) behalf	Accessio
You have full powers to *act* . . .	Accingo

Address.   (Refer to Telegram.)

Registered telegraphic *address* is — . .	Accio
What is your registered telegraphic *address*	Accipio

Agree to your plans . . . . .

Agree to your plans	Accitus
Agree to your proposals	Acclamo
Agree to your request	Acclinis
Agree to your terms	Accola

May I *agree* to —	Accolens
Will you *agree* to —	Accredo

Agreement is arranged as to terms, but waits
    signature   .   .   .   .   .   .   Accresco
Agreement must be sent for our signature .   Accretus
Agreement will be sent for your signature
    to-day .   .   .   .   .   .   Accudo
Agreement will be sent on —   .   .   .   Accumbo
Do you confirm the *agreement*   .   .   .   Accumulo
Have not entered into any *agreement* .   .   Accursus
Have you entered into any *agreement* .   .   Acerbe
They confirm the *agreement*   .   .   .   Acerra
They do not confirm the *agreement*   .   .   Acetaria
We confirm the *agreement* .   .   .   .   Achates
We do not confirm the *agreement*   .   .   Acheron

Alarmed at not having any news   .   .   .   Achnas
Is there any cause for *alarm*   .   .   .   Acidulus

Allowance is asked for of — .   .   .   .   Acinaces
Allowance is too great   .   .   .   .   Acinosus
Allowance is too small   .   .   .   .   Aclis
Have had to make a large *allowance* .   .   Aconitum
Have had to make a small *allowance* .   .   Acopum
What *allowance* is asked for   .   .   .   Acquievi
What *allowance* will you make .   .   .   Acquiro
What *allowance* would you propose   .   .   Acredula

(Alongside)—Expected to be *alongside* by — .   Acriter

Alteration cannot be made .   .   .   .   Acritude
Alteration has been made as requested .   Acroama
Alteration must be made .   .   .   .   Acroasis
Alteration must not be made .   .   .   Actito
No *alteration* has been made .   .   .   Actuosus

What *alteration* has been made . . **Actus**
What *alteration* is asked for . . . **Actutum**
Will make no *alteration* whatever . . . **Aculeus**

Am entirely in your hands . . . . **Acumen**
Am I to take charge of — . . . **Acutulus**
Am leaving town, but will see you on —. **Adactio**
Am quite well, and coming on at once . **Adaggero**
Am quite well, and writing by post . . **Adalligo**
Am very unwell, come as soon as you
can . . . . **Adamo**
Am very unwell, unable to leave to-day . **Adambulo**

Amount is not large enough . . . **Adaperio**
Amount is too large . . . . . **Adaquo**
Amount offered is — . . . . **Adauctus**
Are they good for the *amount* . . **Adaugeo**
Cannot obtain increase of *amount* . . **Adauxi**
Cannot obtain payment of *amount* . . **Adaxint**
Cannot obtain reduction of *amount* . . **Adbibo**
Have sent the *amount* . . . **Addecet**
Have you sent the *amount* . . . **Addenseo**
What *amount* is offered . . . **Addictio**
What will it *amount* to . . . . **Addisco**
Will send the *amount* . . . . **Additus**
Will you send the *amount* . . . **Addivino**

Announcement is confirmed . . . . **Addubito**
Announcement is contradicted . . . **Adduco**
Announcement is doubted . . . . **Adegi**
Announcement is made officially . . **Ademptio**
Announcement is made privately . . **Adeps**
Announcement is made publicly . . . **Adequito**
Announcement is premature . . . **Adesurio**
Announcement is quite true . . . . **Adesus**
Announcement is untrue . . . . **Adeuntis**

Confirm the *announcement*	.	.	.	Adfrango
Contradict the *announcement*		.	.	Adgemo

Annoyed very much at delay	.	.	.	Adhalo
Annoyed very much at refusal		.	.	Adhibeo
Annoyed very much at silence	.		.	Adhinnio
Annoyed very much at statement		.	.	Adhortor

Anxious about safety of —	.	.	.	Adhuc
Anxious to have your reply immediately		.		Adiantum
Anxious to hear from you about —		.	.	Adimo

Anticipate little difficulty	.	.	.	Adipatum
Anticipate much difficulty	.	.	.	Adipsos
Anticipate some difficulty	.	.	.	Aditur
Do you *anticipate* any difficulty	.	.		Aditurus

Apartments requested are secured at — .	Adjaceo
Apartments required are engaged, and ready for immediate occupation	Adjugo
Apartments required are engaged, and will be ready for occupation on —	Adjunctio
Cannot secure *apartments* you wish .	Adjunxi
Cannot secure *apartments* you wish, but can get —	Adjutor
Secure *apartments* at — .	Adjutrix
Secure a bedroom for me .	Admetior
Secure a bedroom and sitting-room .	Admiror
Secure two bedrooms for — .	Admisceo
Secure two bedrooms and sitting-room .	Admistus
Secure three bedrooms .	Admitto
Secure three bedrooms and sitting-room .	Admodum
Secure a double-bedded room . .	Admolior
Secure a double-bedded room and sitting-room	Admoneo
Secure sufficient accommodation for us .	Admordeo

Apply at once for —   .   .   .   .   Admorsus

Do not *apply* for —   .   .   .   .   Admugio

Appointments.   (Refer to CALL, COME, DE-
TAIN, EXPECT, FORGET, MEET, POST-
PONE, TRAIN, WEATHER.)

Appointment has been made for —.   .   . Admutilo

Cannot attend the *appointment* made .   . Adnascor

Cannot keep my *appointment* for —   .   . Adnavigo

What *appointment* has been made   .   . Adnoto

   Hope to be with you in a few days   . Adoptio

   Hope to be with you next week   .   . Adoreus

   Hope to be with you on —   .   . Adorno

   Hope to be with you this evening .   . Adpluo

   Hope to be with you to-day .   . .Adrepo

   Hope to be with you to-morrow   .   . Adscisco

   Hope to see you this evening   .   . Adscitus

   Hope to see you to-day .   .   . Adsum

   Hope to see you to-morrow .   . Advectio

Shall be at home this evening   .   . Advenio

Shall be at office to-day   .   .   . Adventus

Shall be at office to-morrow .   .   . Adversor

Shall be at your house this evening . Adverstm.

Shall be at your house to-day .   . Advexi

Shall be at your office to-day   .   . Advigilo

Shall be at your office to-morrow .   . Adulator

Shall be in town and will see you on —. Adulor

Shall be in town to-day and will call on

   you at —   .   .   .   . Adumbro·

Shall be in town to-morrow and will call

   on you at —   .   .   .   . Aduncus

Shall expect you this evening   .   . Advoco

Shall expect you to-day   .   .   . Advolvo

Shall expect you to-morrow .   .   . Adustio

   Wish to see you, and will remain here until— Adytum

B

Wish to see you, and will remain here until you come	Affabre
Wish to see you. Shall I come? Telegraph reply	Affeci
Wish to see you on business . . .	Affectio
Wish to see you on business. Can you come here? Telegraph . . .	Affero
Wish to see you on business. Make an appointment	Affinis
Wish to see you on business. Please wait my arrival	Affirmo
Wish to see you on business. Shall be here until —	Affixi
Wish to see you on business. Shall be with you about —	Affixus
Wish to see you particularly. Can I see you if I call	Afflatus
Wish to see you particularly. Please come here if possible . . .	Affluo
Wish to see you particularly. Please wait my arrival	Affodio
Wish to see you particularly. Shall be here until —	Afforem
Wish to see you particularly. Telegraph time and place	Affrango
Wish to see you particularly. Will be with you about —	Affremo
Wish to see you this evening, call here .	Affrico
Wish to see you this evening, will call on you	Affulgeo
Wish to see you this morning, call here .	Agaricon
Wish to see you this morning, will call on you	Agedum
Wish to see you to-day	Agellus
Wish to see you to-day, telegraph where	Agema
Wish to see you, will be with you at — .	Agesis

Apprehend the worst . . . . . Agger
    There is little cause for *apprehension* . . Aggestus
    There is no cause for *apprehension* . . Aggravo

Arranged everything satisfactorily, return at
    once . . . . Agilis
    Will *arrange* everything to your satisfaction Agilitas

Arrangement has been made . . . . Agitator
    Arrangement has fallen through . . . Agnascor
    Arrangement still under discussion . . Agnatio
    Can you come to any *arrangement* . . Agnos
    Make some definite *arrangement* . . . Agnosco
    What *arrangement* do you propose . . Agnovi
    What *arrangement* is come to . . . Agrarius
    What *arrangement* is suggested . . . Agrestis
    Will not make any *arrangement* . . . Agria

Arrival. (Refer to Goods, Home, Hotels, Train.)
    Arrival is expected on the — . . . Agricola
    Cannot account for non-*arrival*. Will make
      immediate enquiry . . . . Agripeta
    Enquire of agents date of *arrival* . . Agrium
    Enquire of agents date and port of *arrival* . Ahenipes
    Enquire of agents date and port of *arrival*,
      and meet me . . . . . Aizoon
    Glad to hear of your safe *arrival* . . Alabaster
    Shall *arrive* about — . . . . Alacer
    Shall *arrive* and require a conveyance at —. Alacritas
    Shall *arrive* and require a porter at — . Alapa
    Shall *arrive* and require breakfast at — . Alatus
    Shall *arrive* and require dinner at — . . Alauda
    Shall *arrive* and require lunch at — . . Albarius
    Shall *arrive* and require supper at — . . Albesco
    Shall *arrive* and require tea — . . . Albor
    Arrived here after a very bad passage . . Albumen

Arrived here after a very good passage .	Alburnum
Arrived here, all in good order . . .	Alcedo
Arrived here all well	Algensis
Arrived here all well, health much improved.	Algidus
Arrived here all well, very tired . . .	Algor
Arrived here all well, I will write to-day .	Algosus
Arrived here all well, I will write to-morrow	Alias
Arrived here all well, leave again to-day .	Alica
Arrived here all well, leave again to-morrow	Alicubi
Arrived here all well, leave for — . .	Alienatio
Arrived here all well, leave for home — .	Alienus
Arrived here all well, leave for home to-day	Alifer
Arrived here all well, leave for home to-morrow	Alimon
Arrived here all well, meet me at — .	Alioqui
Arrived here all well, remain to-night . .	Aliorsum
Arrived here all well, remain until —. .	Altitudo
Arrived here all well, wait my arrival . .	Altrix
Arrived here unwell, meet me at — . .	Alveare
Ascertain the reason and telegraph at once .	Alveolus
Ascertain the reason and write at once .	Alveus
Assistance is not required	Alum
Assistance is urgently required . . .	Amabilis
Ask for what *assistance* you require . .	Amando
Cannot render any *assistance* . . .	Amarus
Will give all the *assistance* in our power .	Amasius
(Avoid)—Do your best to *avoid* — . . .	Amator
Do your utmost to *avoid* any unpleasantness	Amatrix
Bank rate has been raised —	Ambedo
——— ¼ per cent.	Ambesus
——— ½ per cent. . . . . · .	Ambique
——— ¾ per cent.	Ambio
——— 1 per cent. . ·. . .	Ambustio

Bank rate has been reduced — . . .	Amellus
——— ¼ per cent.	Amentia
——— ½ per cent.	Amerina
——— ¾ per cent.	Amicitia
——— 1 per cent.	Amiculum

Bankruptcy petition has been filed by —. .	Amissio
Bankruptcy proceedings have been taken against —	Ammium

Bills. (Refer to ACCEPTANCE.)

Bills of Lading are not yet made out . .	Ammonis
Bills of Lading are sent by this mail . .	Amnicola
Bills of Lading have not been endorsed .	Amolior
Bills of Lading will be sent by next mail .	Amomis
Have you sent *Bills of Lading* . . .	Ampelos
How are *Bills of Lading* forwarded . .	Amphora
How are *Bills of Lading* made out . .	Amplio
Send *Bills of Lading* immediately . .	Amplius

(Births)—Confined this morning, *Boy*, both doing well	Ampulla
Confined this morning, *Boy*, dead, Mother well	Amputo
Confined this morning, *Girl*, both doing well	Amuletum
Confined this morning, *Girl*, dead, Mother well	Amusium
Confined to-day, Baby dead, Mother fairly well	Amussis
Confined to-day, Baby dead, Mother weak .	Amygdala
Confined to-day, Baby dead, Mother very weak	Amylon
Confined to-day, Baby dead, Mother fairly well, will telegraph again	Amystis

Confined to-day, Baby dead, Mother weak, will telegraph again	Anatinus
Confined to-day, Baby dead, Mother very weak, will telegraph again . . .	Anceps
Confined to-day, *Twins*, both *boys*, all well .	Ancilium
Confined to-day, *Twins*, both *girls*, all well .	Ancilla
Confined to-day, *Twins, boy and girl*, all well	Ancon
Confined to-day, *Twins*, one alive, a *boy*, Mother well.	Andabata
Confined to-day, *Twins*, one alive, a *boy*, Mother weak	Andron
Confined to-day, *Twins*, one alive, a *boy*, Mother not expected to live . . .	Anellus
Confined to-day, *Twins*, one alive, a *girl*, Mother well	Anemone
Confined to-day, *Twins*, one alive, a *girl*, Mother weak	Anethum
Confined to-day, *Twins*, one alive, a *girl*, Mother not expected to live . .	Angina
Confined to-day, *Twins*, both dead, Mother well	Anguifer
Confined to-day, *Twins*, both dead, Mother weak	Anguinus
Confined to-day, *Twins*, both dead, Mother not expected to live	Anguipes
Confined yesterday, *Boy*, both doing well .	Anguis
Confined yesterday, *Boy*, dead, Mother well.	Angulus
Confined yesterday, *Boy*, dead, Mother fairly well	Angustia
Confined yesterday, *Girl*, both doing well .	Anhelo
Confined yesterday, *Girl*, dead, Mother well	Anicetum
Confined yesterday, *Girl*, dead, Mother fairly well	Aniciana
Confined yesterday, *Twins*, both *boys*, all well	Anilis
Confined yesterday, *Twins*, both *girls*, all well	Animalis

Confined yesterday, *Twins, boy and girl,* all
well . . . . **Animatio**

Confined yesterday, *Twins,* one alive, a *boy,*
Mother well. . . . . **Animor**

Confined yesterday, *Twins,* one alive, a *boy,*
Mother weak . . . . **Animosus**

Confined yesterday, *Twins,* one alive, a *boy,*
Mother not expected to live . . . **Anisum**

Confined yesterday, *Twins,* one alive, a *girl,*
Mother well . . . . . **Annalis**

Confined yesterday, *Twins,* one alive, a *girl,*
Mother weak . . . . **Annavigo**

Confined yesterday, *Twins,* one alive, a *girl,*
Mother not expected to live . . . **Annexus**

Confined yesterday, *Twins,* both dead, Mother
well . . . . **Annifer**

Confined yesterday, *Twins,* both dead, Mother
weak . . . . **Annona**

Confined yesterday, *Twins,* both dead, Mother
not expected to live . . . . **Annosus**

Book is not yet published . . . . **Annumero**
Book is not published by us . . . **Annuntio**
Book is out of print . . . . **Anodyna**
The published price of the *book* is — . **Anonium**
Book will be published about —. . **Anormis**
Last edition of *book* completely sold out . **Ansatus**
New edition of *book* will be ready — . **Anteago**

Bring home or order from— . . . **Antecedo**
Bring home or order from the Stores — . **Antefero**
Bring home or send at once — . . . **Antenna**
Bring home with you — . . . **Antepono**
Bring home with you from — . . **Antequam**
Bring home with you from the Stores — . **Antesto**

Bring some fish with you to-day . . .	Antetuli
Bring some fruit with you to-day . .	Antevolo
Bring some game with you to-day . .	Anthedon
Bring with you when next you come . .	Anthera

Business. (Refer to HEALTH.)

Business is suspended on account of holidays	Anthrax
Business will be entertained . . .	Anticipo
Cannot be at *business* to-day . . .	Anticus
Cannot be at *business* to-day ; am suffering from an attack of —	Antidotum
Cannot be at *business* to-day ; bring letters, &c., here	Antistes
Cannot be at *business* to-day ; send anything requiring my attention here . . .	Antlia
Cannot be at *business* to-day ; send clerk with letters, telegrams, &c. . . .	Antrum
Cannot be at *business* to-day ; send messenger with letters, &c.	Anxietas
Cannot be at *business* to-day ; too unwell .	Anxifer
Cannot be at *business* to-day ; unnecessary to send messenger, but post letters . .	Anxiferum
Cannot be at *business* to-day until late .	Apage
Cannot be at *business* for a few days . .	Apagesis
Cannot be at *business* for a few days ; letter by post	Apathes
Do not do the *business*	Apecula
Do you consider the *business* sound . .	Aperio
When will *business* be concluded . .	Apertura

Buy for me on best terms . . . . | Apexabo |
Can *buy* at —	Aphaca
Can *buy* more on same terms . .	Aplustre
Can you *buy* —	Apocynon
Can you *buy* at	Apolecti

Can you *buy* more on same terms . .	Apologus
Cannot *buy* at —	Apostema
Cannot *buy* more	Apotheca
Do not *buy*	Appareo
Do not *buy* any more	Appendix
What price can you *buy* at . . .	Appendo
What price did you *buy* at . . .	Appensus
What quantity can you *buy* . .	Appeto
What quantity did you *buy* . .	Appiana

Call at once upon —	Applaudo
Call at post office for letters . .	Apporto
Call at this address	Appositus
Call here on your way to business .	Appotus
Call here on your way from business .	Apprime
Call here to-day if possible . .	Apprimus
Call here to-day, without fail . .	Appulsus
Call on me at my office . . .	Aprilis
Call on me at my office at once . .	Apronia
Do not *call* upon	Aprugnus
Calling on you to-day . . .	Apsis
Calling on you to-day on an important matter	Apsyctos
Calling on you to-day on important business	Apyrinus
Calling on you to-day with reference to — .	Apyrum
Calling on you to-day as desired . .	Aqua

Cancel. (Refer to TELEGRAM.)	
Cancel my previous telegram, and substitute following	Aquator
Cancel orders already given respecting — .	Aquosus
Cancel orders at any cost, reply by telegram	Arabilis
Cancel orders if not already attended to .	Aranea
Cancel orders if not already attended to, letter follows	Araneola
Cancel orders in my telegram . .	Aratrum

Cancel orders in my telegram, letter by post   **Arbiter**
Cancel orders in my letter .   .   .   .   **Arbitror**
Cancel orders previously sent, and substitute
    following — .   .   .   .   **Arboreus**
Cancel orders, wait further instructions   .   **Arbusto**
Cannot *cancel* orders, already attended to .   **Arbustum**
Cannot *cancel* orders already attended to,
    letter follows .   .   .   .   .   **Arbuteus**

Carriage must be charged forward .   .   .   **Arcanus**
Carriage must be prepaid .   .   .   .   **Archon**
Carriage must be sent for me   .   .   **Arctos**
Carriage need not be sent for me   .   .   **Arcturus**

Charge has been made in error   .   .   **Arcuatim**
Charge has been withdrawn   .   .   **Ardelio**
Am I to take *charge* of — .   .   .   **Ardenter**
Take charge of — .   .   .   **Ardesco**
Take charge of everything .   .   .   **Arduitas**
Take charge of everything until my arrival .   **Arefacio**
Whom do you wish to take *charge* of —   .   **Arenosus**
Charges must be paid by — .   .   **Arenula**
Shall I pay *charges* .   .   .   .   **Areola**
Who will pay the *charges* .   .   .   **Argema**

Cheque.   (Refer to Money, Remittance.)
Cheque is sent to-day .   .   .   .   **Argemone**
Cheque has been duly paid .   .   .   **Argentum**
Cheque has been lost. Stop payment .   **Argilla**
Cheque has been presented and paid .   **Argus**
Cheque has been presented and returned
    marked — .   .   .   .   .   .   **Arguto**
Cheque returned unpaid, send cash by return
    of post .   .   .   .   .   **Argyritis**
Cheque will be sent to-morrow .   .   **Ariditas**
Has *cheque* been paid .   .   .   .   **Arieto**

Has *cheque* been sent	Aritudo
How was *cheque* sent . . .	Armarium
Make *cheque* payable to bearer . .	Armatura
Make *cheque* payable to our order .	Armifer
Send uncrossed *cheque* payable to bearer .	Aroma

Christmas greetings to you	Arrectus

Circumstances beyond my control compel me to decline	Arrexi
Circumstances beyond my control prevent my accepting	Arrhabo
Under no *circumstances* . . .	Arripio
What are the *circumstances* of the case .	Arrisor

Claim has been allowed	Arsurus
Claim has been disallowed . . .	Artemon
Send us particulars of the *claim* . .	Arteria

Come as soon as you can . . .	Articulo
Can you *come* here	Arvalis
Cannot *come* to-day	Arvina
Cannot *come* to-night, accept my apologies .	Aruspex
Cannot *come* until —	Asarum
Do not *come*	Asbolus
Do not *come*, am leaving for home .	Ascendo
Do not *come*, reasons by letter . .	Ascopera
Do not *come* until you get my letter .	Ascribo
Do not *come* until — . . .	Asellus
Glad to hear you are *coming* . .	Asinarius
Glad to hear you are *coming*, will meet you	Asotus

Commence as soon as possible . . .	Aspecto
Cannot *commence* before . . .	Aspergo
When do you *commence* . . .	Aspernor

Commission must be provided for of — . . Aspexi
   Commission will be allowed of — . . Aspicio
   What *commission* will be allowed . . Aspiro

Communication by telephone is interrupted . Asplenon
   Address all *communications* to — . . Asporto
   In *communication* with — . . . . Aspretum
   In *communication* respecting the — . . Assecla

Compliments of the season . . . . Assector
   Compliments of the season to all from all here Assensio

Comply with their requirements as far as you can Assequor
   Comply with their requirements in all respects Assero
   Comply with their requirements under protest Assessor
   Cannot *comply* with your wishes . . Assevero
   Will *comply* with your wishes . . . Assicco

Compromise, if you think it desirable . . Assideo
   Compromise on the terms indicated . . Assigno
   Compromise upon any terms . . . Assimulo
   Do not *compromise* . . . . . Assisto

Concerts. (See Theatres and Concerts.)

Conclude negotiations at once, or break off . Associo
   Have you come to any *conclusion* . . Assolet

Condole with you in our mutual great loss . Assuesco
   Condole with you in your great loss . . Assulose

Confidential agent will be sent on our behalf . Assulto
   Following is strictly *confidential* . . Assyrius

Congratulate you on the birth of a daughter . Astaphis
   Congratulate you on the birth of a son . Asterion
   Congratulate you on the happy event . . Asterno

Congratulate you on the well-merited honour	Astituo
Congratulate you on your appointment .	Astrepo
Congratulate you on your birthday . .	Astrifer
Congratulate you on your good fortune .	Astringo
Congratulate you on your marriage .	Astrum
Congratulate you on your promotion . .	Astruxi
Congratulate you on your safe arrival . .	Asturco
Congratulate you on your success . .	Atavus

Conjoint action is advisable	Athara
Are you acting in *conjunction* . . .	Atheroma

Consequences will be very serious . . .	Athleta
It is of great *consequence*	Atocium
It is of no *consequence*	Atricolor

Consideration must be given to the proposal .	Atriolum
Cannot reply without further *consideration* .	Atriplex

Consignment duly despatched . . .	Atrium
Consignment duly received	Atrophia
How is it *consigned*	Attactus

Consult some authority in the matter . .	Attagen
Consult some authority in the matter and let me know result	Attestor
Consult your business agent . . .	Attexo
Consult your business agent and let me know result	Atthis
Consult your friends	Attollo
Consult your friends and let me know result	Attonite
Consult your legal adviser	Attonsus
Consult your legal adviser and let me know result	Attractus
Consult your stockbroker	Attraho
Consult your stockbroker and let me know result	Attremo

Have consulted business agent, who says —	Attritus
Have consulted business agent, will post particulars	Auctio
Have consulted friends, who say — .	Aucupium
Have consulted friends, will post you particulars	Audacia
Have consulted legal adviser, who says — .	Audax
Have consulted legal adviser, will post particulars	Audenter
Have consulted stockbroker, who says — .	Auditio
Have consulted stockbroker, will post particulars	Aufero
Cannot attend the *consultation* . . .	Aufugio
When is the *consultation* fixed for . .	Augesco

Continue to advise fully by letter . . .	Augmen
Continue to advise fully by telegram . .	Augurium
Continue the negotiation	Auletes

(Convenient)—It is quite *convenient* . . .	Aureolus
It is not *convenient*	Auresco
Whichever is most *convenient* . . .	Auricula
Will it be *convenient* to	Aurifex

Cost is estimated at —	Auriga
Cost must not exceed —	Auritus
Cannot estimate *cost*	Aurora

Countermand the order at once . . .	Ausculto
It has been *countermanded* . . .	Auspicor

Country post has been delayed . . .	Austerus
Will reply on my return from the *country* .	Avaritia
Will telegraph on arrival in the *country* .	Avarus
Will write on arrival in the *country* .	Aveho
— is in the *country*, will communicate with him and then reply	Caballus

Damage is serious	Cacabus
Damage is slight	Cachexia
How long will it take to repair *damage*	Cachinno
How was *damage* caused	Cachla
What is amount of *damage* done . . .	Cadaver
Date of last letter is —	Cadivus
What *date* do you arrive . . .	Cadmites
What *date* do you leave . . .	Caduceum
What *date* does trial commence . .	Caelamen
What *date* does your leave commence .	Caelum
What *date* does your leave terminate .	Calcitro
What *date* was your last letter . .	Calefacio
What *date* was your last telegram .	Caligo
Day after to-morrow	Callidus
How many *days* can you allow . .	Calthula
In the course of the *day* . . .	Calvaria
In the course of the last few *days* .	Calvatus
In the course of the next few *days* .	Calyx
Dealt with them for many years . .	Camella
(Deaths)—When did he (or she) *die* .	Camera
Died suddenly, come at once . .	Caminor
Died suddenly, do not come, will write you.	Cancello
Died suddenly, require instructions .	Cancer
Died suddenly, will write particulars .	Candela
Died to-day, come at once . . .	Candesco
Died to-day, do not come, will write .	Canicula
Died to-day, will write particulars .	Canopus
Died yesterday, come at once . .	Cantamen
Died yesterday, do not come, will write	Cantator
Died yesterday, will write particulars .	Canticum
Baby died to-day, particulars by letter .	Capedo
Baby died yesterday, particulars by letter .	Capella

Daughter died to-day, particulars by letter .	Capistro
Daughter died yesterday, particulars by letter	Capitium
Father died to-day, come at once　.　.	Capnitis
Father died to-day, do not come, will write you　.　.　.　.　.　.　.	Cappa
Father died yesterday, particulars by letter .	Capsula
Father died to-day, particulars by letter　.	Captatio
Grandchild died to-day, will write you　.	Captiose
Grandchild died yesterday, will write you .	Captus
Grandfather died to-day, will write you　.	Carbasus
Grandfather died yesterday, will write you .	Carbo
Grandmother died to-day, will write you　.	Cardisce
Grandmother died yesterday, will write you.	Carectum
Husband died to-day, come at once　.　.	Carmino
Husband died to-day, do not come, will write you　.　.　.　.　.　.	Carnifex
Husband died to-day, particulars by letter .	Carphos
Husband died yesterday, particulars by letter	Carpinus
Mother died to-day, come at once　.　.	Carptim
Mother died to-day, do not come, will write you　.　.　.　.　.　.	Carruca
Mother died to-day, particulars by letter　.	Caryotis
Mother died yesterday, particulars by letter.	Casia
Sister died to-day, come at once .　.　.	Cassida
Sister died to-day, do not come, will write you	Castanea
Sister died to-day, particulars by letter　.	Castigo
Sister died yesterday, particulars by letter .	Castus
Son died to-day, come at once　.　.　.	Catasta
Son died to-day, do not come, will write you	Cathedra
Son died to-day, particulars by letter .　.	Catillus
Son died yesterday, particulars by letter　.	Caucon
Wife died to-day, come at once .　.　.	Caudex
Wife died to-day, do not come, will write you	Caupona
Wife died to-day, particulars by letter　.	Causatio
Wife died yesterday, particulars by letter .	Cautim
Take charge of all *effects*, letter by post　.	Cavator

Funeral takes place at —	Caveo
Funeral takes place on the — . . .	Cedo
Funeral takes place and trust you will come on the —	Cedratus
When does *funeral* take place . . .	Cedrium
Send me a lock of his (or her) *hair* . .	Celeber
Will cannot be found	Cellula
Will cannot be found, can you give any information	Celsus
Has made a *Will* which is now in the custody of —	Cenchris
Has made no *Will*	Censio

Decision. (Refer to FINAL.)

Decision may be expected about — . .	Centrum
When will it be *decided*	Centuria

Decline to accept . . . . . . Cepa

Decline to accept, except on terms proposed.	Cepetum
Decline to accept, except on terms already mentioned	Cephalus
Decline to accept on any conditions . .	Cepphus
Decline to accept on terms mentioned . .	Cepurica
Decline to accept the responsibility . .	Ceraria
Decline to accept under any circumstances .	Cerastes

Deduction proposed is agreed to . . . Ceratium

No *deduction* can be allowed . . .	Cerberus
Will pay on *deduction*	Cerealis

Delay departure . . . . . . Cerifico

Delay departure until you receive my letter	Cerno
Delay departure until you hear again . .	Ceroma
Cannot be longer *delayed*	Cerritus
Further *delay* is unnecessary . . .	Certamen
Is any *delay* likely to occur . . .	Cervix

C

It was unavoidably *delayed*   . . .   Cestus
There will be considerable *delay* . . .   Cetarius
There will be some *delay* . . . .   Chalcis

Deliver only against payment   . . .   Chaos
Can only *deliver* on prepayment . . .   Charta
Cannot be *delivered* owing to insufficient
     address   . . . . .   Chelonia
Cannot *deliver* the goods by the time
     named   . . . . .   Chelys
Cannot *deliver* the goods until —   . .   Chersos
Do not *deliver* until you receive instruc-
     tions . . . . . .   Chia
Delivery can be made at once   . . .   Chimaera
Delivery can be made in —   . . .   Chlamys

Departure.   (Refer to DELAY, DETAINED,
     EMBARKING, LEAVING, PASSAGE, TRAIN,
     WEATHER.)
Departure postponed . . . . .   Chlorion
Departure postponed until —   . . .   Chorus
Departure postponed until next mail . .   Chreston
Departure postponed for a few days . .   Chroma
Departure postponed for one month . .   Chrysos
Departure postponed for one month, letter
     follows   . . . . . .   Cibalis
Departure postponed for six weeks . .   Ciborium
Departure postponed for six weeks, letter
     follows   . . . . . .   Cicatrix
Departure postponed for two months . .   Cicera
Departure postponed for two months, letter
     follows   . . . . .   Ciconia

Describe exactly what you want   . . .   Cimex
Describe the position fully . . . .   Cimolia

Send us detailed *description* . . . Cinctura
We must have better *description* . . Cingulum

Despatch is of utmost importance . . . Ciniflo
Cannot be *despatched* before — . . . Circa
When will you *despatch* . . . . Circiter
Will be *despatched* by — . . . . Circulus
Has been already *despatched* . . . Circumdo

Detained here . . . . . . Cisium
Detained here by contrary winds, will advise
    departure . . . . . . Cista
Detained here by heavy gale, will advise
    departure . . . . . . Cistifer
Detained here, cannot return to-day . . Citerior
Detained here, cannot return to-night . . Cithara
Detained here, do not expect me . . Citimus
Detained here, do not expect me until — . Citrum
Detained here, do not wait . . . Civicus
Detained here, do not wait, will follow . Clamito
Detained here, expect me about — . . Clamor
Detained here, expect to leave about — . Clango
Detained here owing to private affairs . Clathro
Detained here, shall be with you later . . Clavulus
Detained here, shall dine at the club . . Clemens
Detained here, shall not be home to dinner . Clepere
Detained here, will return — . . . Clibanus
Detained here, will return to-night . . Clinamen
Detained here, will return to-morrow . . Clinice
Detained here for a few days . . . Clivina
Detained here for a few days, letter by post . Clivosus
Detained here until next mail . . . Cloaca
Detained here until next mail, letter by post Cludo

Difficulties. (Refer to Anticipate.)
Difficult to carry out your requirements . Clunis
c 2

Difficulties exist, but they may be overcome	Clypeus
Difficulties exist which cannot be overcome .	Coactio
Do any *difficulties* exist . . .	Coactus
Diligence is of greatest importance . . .	Coaggero
Diligence shall be exercised . . .	Coagulum
Dimensions in detail must be sent us . .	Coalesco
(Dinner Engagements)—*Accept* your invitation to *dine*	Coarcto
Accept your invitation to *dine*, and will call at —	Coaxatio
Accept your invitation to *dine*, and will wait here for you	Coccinus
— *dines* with us this evening . . .	Cocles
— *dines* with us this evening, and remains the night	Coctivus
— *dines* with us this evening, but leaves early	Codex
— *dines* with us this evening, shall leave it entirely to you	Coetus
— *dines* with us this evening, will be glad if you will join us . . .	Cognatus
Dining out this evening, do not expect me until —	Cognomen
Dining out this evening, send my dress clothes here	Cognosco
Dining out this evening, send my dress clothes to —	Cohors
Dining out this evening, will join you at —	Cohortor
Dining out this evening with — . .	Colaphus
Received *invitation* to dine with — . .	Collabor
Received *invitation* to dine and Theatre this evening with —	Collaria
Received *invitation* to dine and Theatre, can you come	Collaudo

Received *invitation* to dine and Theatre, shall I accept	Collectio
Will dine with you on the — . . .	Collido .
Will dine with you to-day	Colloco
Will dine with you to-day, and wait your arrival at —	Collum
Will dine with you to-day, and call at — .	Collybus
Will dine with you to-morrow . . .	Collyra
Will dine with you to-morrow, and wait for you	Colonia
Will dine with you to-morrow, and call for you	Colorate
Will dine with you on Monday . . .	Colossus
Will dine with you on Tuesday . . .	Columba
Will dine with you on Wednesday . .	Colurnus
Will dine with you on Thursday . .	Coluthea
Will dine with you on Friday . . .	Comatus
Will dine with you on Saturday. . .	Comicus
Will dine with you on Sunday . . .	Comitium
Will you dine with me — . . .	Commadeo
Will you dine with me to-day at — . .	Commigro
Will you dine with me to-day, will call on you at —	Committo
Will you dine with me to-day at the Club at —	Commode
Will you dine with me to-day, and call for me at —	Commorit
Will you dine with me to-day here at — .	Commuto
Will you dine with me to-day with a few friends, at —	Compactio
Will you dine with me to-morrow at — .	Compago
Will you dine with me to-morrow at the Club, at —	Compasco
Will you dine with me to-morrow here at —	Compedis
Will you dine with me to-morrow with a few friends, at —	Compello

Will you dine with me to-morrow, will call on you at —	Compingo
Will you dine with me to-morrow, and call for me at —.	Compitum
Will you dine with me on Monday at — .	Complano
Will you dine with me on Tuesday at — .	Complico
Will you dine with me on Wednesday at —	Compos
Will you dine with me on Thursday at — .	Comprimo
Will you dine with me on Friday at — .	Comptus
Will you dine with me on Saturday at — .	Concivi
Will you dine with me on Sunday at —. .	Conclamo
Will you dine with me on the — . .	Concluse
Directions have been given	Concolor
What *directions* have been given . .	Concoquo
Disbursements amount to —	Conculco
Send full account of *disbursements* . .	Concumbo
What do *disbursements* amount to . .	Condemno
Dispatch. (See D**ESPATCH**.)	
Dispose of it as you please	Condoleo
Please hold at *disposal* of — . . .	Condris
Would they be *disposed* to — . . .	Conduxi
Dispute has arisen between —. . . .	Condylus
There is no *dispute*	Confero
What is the cause of the *dispute*. . .	Confisus
(Distance)—What is the *distance* . . .	Conformo
Do as you propose	Confusus
Do as you think best	Congelo
Do your utmost for our joint benefit . .	Congeries
Do your utmost in the matter . . .	Congius

Do your utmost on my behalf . . .	Conglobo
Have *done* as you requested . . .	Congruo

Doctor. (Refer to HEALTH, MEDICINE.)

Documents. (Refer to ACKNOWLEDGE.)

Documents are signed. What is to be done with them	Congruum
Documents for your signature have been forwarded	Conifer
Documents for your signature have been forwarded by registered letter . . .	Coniferum
Documents signed and returned you . .	Conisso
Documents signed and posted to-day . .	Conjugo
Documents will be signed — . . .	Conjux
Documents will be signed and sent you — .	Connexus

(Effort)—Every *effort* has been made . .	Conopeum

(Elsewhere)—Shall I try *elsewhere* . .	Conquiro

Embarking on board the —	Conscius
When do you *embark*	Conseco

Empower you to act for me . . .	Consepio
— is *empowered* to act	Consisto
Is he *empowered* to act . . .	Consolor
— is not *empowered* to act . . .	Consors.

(Enclosure)—Send for *enclosure* to-day to — .	Conspuo
Send for *enclosure* to-morrow to — .	Consulto

Enquire fully and report by letter . .	Contagio
Enquire fully and report by telegram .	Contendo
Enquire of agents respecting — . .	Continuo

Enquire of carriers	Contorsi
Enquire of railway company . . .	Contra
Have made enquiries	Contremo
Have made enquiries and will post you result	Contumax
Have made enquiries of agents, who say —	Contundo
Have made enquiries of carriers, who say —.	Convecto
Have made enquiries of railway company, who say —	Converse
Erection is proceeding rapidly . . .	Convexi
Erection is proceeding slowly . . .	Conviva
How is *erection* proceeding . . .	Convoco
How long will *erection* take . . .	Convolvo
Error has arisen	Conus
It is a clerical *error*	Coopto
(Essential)—Do you consider it *essential* . .	Coquino
It is most *essential*	Coram
It is not *essential*	Corbula
Estimates cannot be furnished before — . .	Corculus
Estimate has been accepted . . .	Cordyla
Estimate has been rejected	Cornipes
Estimated loss is —	Corolla
Estimated profit is —	Corpus
Estimates are high	Corrado
Estimates are low	Corsa
Estimates will be sent on by — . .	Cosmeta
Can you give us an *estimate* . .	Cotoneum
What is the *estimated* value of — . .	Cottana
Everything arranged	Coturnix
Everything left entirely to you . .	Crabro

Examination will take place on the — . . Crapula
   Failed in the *Examination* . . . . Crassus
   Passed successfully in the *Examination* . Crates

Exception cannot be made . . . . Creatrix
   Exception will be made . . . . Credulus

Executors appointed are — . . . . Crematio
   Who are appointed *executors* . . . Cremo

Expect. (Refer to HEALTH.)
   Expect to be with you — . . . . Crepida
   Expect to be with you this evening . . Crepitus
   Expect to be with you to-morrow . . Cribrum
   Expect to be with you in a few days . . Crispus
   Expect to be with you in time for — . . Croceus
   Am daily *expecting* to receive information . Crocota
   Have been *expecting* letter from my husband.
      Telegraph how he is . . . . . Crudesco
   Have been *expecting* letter from my wife.
      Telegraph how she is . . . . Crudus
   Have been *expecting* letter. Telegraph health
      of — . . . . Crumena
   Have been *expecting* letter. Telegraph how
      you are getting on. . . . . Crusta
   Have been *expecting* letter. Telegraph news Crux
   Have been *expecting* to hear from you . . Crypta
   Have been *expecting* to hear from you. Are
      you well . . . . . . Cubatus
   Have been *expecting* to hear from you. Very
      anxious . . . . . . Cucuma

Expenses to be paid by — . . . . Culearis
   At whose *expense* . . . . . Culminia
   Do your utmost to avoid unnecessary *expense* Cultor

No *expense* must be incurred . . .	Cultrix
Will bear the *expense*.	Cumulate
Experiments have been successful . . .	Cuneo
Experiments have not been successful . .	Cunque
Report result of *experiments* . . .	Cupa
Explanation impossible by telegraph . .	Curculio
Explanation sent by letter	Curiosus
Facilitate matters as much as you can . .	Cursito
Do nothing to *facilitate* them . . .	Curvatio
Shall be happy to offer any *facilities* . .	Custodia
What *facilities* have they for — . .	Cuticula
What *facilities* have you for — . .	Cyamos
Fault has been remedied	Cybium
Fault is entirely theirs . . .	Cyminum
Fault is ours	Cynicus
Fault is not ours	Cynomyla
Fault is yours	Cynosura
What is the nature of the *fault* . .	Cyperis
Was *faulty* when it reached us . .	Dabula
Final decision come to is — . . .	Dactylis
Consider the decision *final* . . .	Daemon
Is your decision to be considered *final* .	Damnatio
Find out all you can, and report . .	Damnose
Where can we *find* — . . .	Danista
Have *found* what is wanted . .	Dapalis
Finish as quickly as possible . . .	Daphne
Finish work at any cost . . .	Dartos
Expect to be *finished* on or about — .	Dasypus
How soon can it be *finished* . .	Datarius

Fire broke out — . . . . . . Dealbo
  Fire broke out this morning . . . Decanto
  Fire broke out to-day, little damage, working
    as usual . . . . , . Decennis
  Fire broke out to-day, great damage . . Decessor
  Fire broke out to-day, great damage, work
    stopped . . . . . Decidium
  Fire broke out to-day, come at once . . Decoctor
  Fire broke out last night . . . . Decollo
  Fire broke out last night, little damage . Decresco
  Fire broke out last night, great damage . Decuria
  Fire broke out last night, still burning . Decursus
  Fire broke out here, place completely destroyed Defamo
  Fire broke out close here, premises in danger Defectio
  Fire broke out close here, premises not in
    danger . . . . . . Deflagro
  Fire broke out in adjoining premises, ours in
    danger . . . . . . Deflexi
  Fire broke out in adjoining premises, ours safe Deformis
  Have had a *fire*, business as usual . . Defossus

Fix a meeting for — . . . . . . Degener
  Fix a meeting for any day convenient to — Deglubo
  What date is the meeting *fixed* for . . Degusto

Follow it up immediately . . . . Dehisco
  The remainder will *follow* by next mail . Deinceps

(Forget)—Do not *forget* — . . . . Delabor
  Do not *forget* to bring — . . . . Delacero
  Do not *forget* to come this evening . . Delego
  Do not *forget* to-night's engagement . . Deletrix
  Do not *forget* your appointment for to-day . Delinquo
  Do not *forget* your appointment for to-morrow Deliro
  Forgotten my bag, please keep until — . Deltoton
  Forgotten my books, please keep until — . Delubrum

Forgotten my box, please keep until — .	Demando
Forgotten my keys, please keep until — .	Demetor
Forgotten my letters, please keep until — .	Demigro
Forgotten my luggage, please keep until —.	Demitto
Forgotten my overcoat, please keep until —.	Demorior
Forgotten my papers, please keep until — .	Denarius
Forgotten my parcel, please keep until — .	Denascor
Forgotten my portmanteau, please keep until	Denique
Forgotten my purse, please keep until — .	Dens
Forgotten my things, please keep until — .	Dentale
Forgotten my umbrella, please keep until —	Dentitio
Forgotten my waterproof, please keep until —	Denudo
Forgotten my bag, please send immediately to —	Denumero
Forgotten my books, please send immediately to —	Depactus
Forgotten my box, please send immediately to —	Dependo
Forgotten my keys, please send immediately to —	Deplumis
Forgotten my letters, please send immediately to —	Depopulo
Forgotten my luggage, please send immediately to —	Deprimo
Forgotten my overcoat, please send immediately to —	Depso
Forgotten my papers, please send immediately to —	Depulsio
Forgotten my parcel, please send immediately to —	Depygis
Forgotten my portmanteau, please send immediately to —	Derosus
Forgotten my purse, please send immediately to—	Derumpo
Forgotten my things, please send immediately to —	Descendo

Forgotten my umbrella, please send immediately to — .   .   .   .   **Describo**

Forgotten my waterproof, please send immediately to — .   .   .   .   **Desertor**

Forward.   (Refer to SEND, LETTERS.)

Forward any communications there may be waiting for me to — .   .   .   **Desidia**

Forward my luggage here .   .   .   .   **Designo**

Forward my luggage to — .   .   .   **Desisto**

Forward my things here .   .   .   .   **Desitum**

Forward my things to — .   .   .   **Despecto**

How have my letters been *forwarded* .   .   **Despicor**

They shall be *forwarded* by next post .   .   **Despolio**

When will you *forward* .   .   .   **Desubito**

Will be *forwarded* immediately .   .   .   **Desuper**

Freight cannot be obtained .   .   .   **Deterius**

Freight has been engaged .   .   .   **Detorno**

Cannot obtain *freight* enough .   .   **Devectus**

What *freight* can you obtain .   .   **Devello**

Funeral.   (Refer to DEATHS.)

Get on quickly with — .   .   .   .   **Dextans**

Get on quickly with work .   .   .   **Diadema**

Glad to hear from you .   .   .   .   **Diallage**

Go as quickly as possible .   .   .   **Diametros**

Go as quickly as possible to — .   .   **Dianome**

Goods.   (Refer to ARRIVAL, INVOICES, ORDER, PATTERN, QUALITY, QUANTITY, SAMPLE, SEND.)

Goods arrived in bad condition .   .   .   **Diapente**

Goods arrived in bad condition; letter follows	Diatoni
Goods arrived safe	Diaulus
Goods arrived slightly damaged; letter follows	Dicatura
Goods left by —	Dictator
Goods not arrived —	Diduco
Goods not arrived; make enquiries . .	Diecula
Goods not arrived; make enquiries. Am doing so here	Diffamo
Goods not arrived; when did they leave .	Diffido
Goods not arrived; when did they leave, and how	Diffuse
Goods on order waiting remittance . .	Digero
Have you received the *goods* . . .	Digestio
Have you received the *goods* sent by — .	Dignosco
Have you received the *goods* sent on the — .	Dijudico
Guarantee must be given	Dilamino
The quality must be *guaranteed* . . .	Dilapsus
Who will *guarantee* us . . .	Dilorico
Will *guarantee* to the extent of — . .	Dilutium
Will you *guarantee* — . . .	Dimadeo
Happy New Year	Dimidius
Happy New Year to all . . .	Diminuo
Happy New Year to all at home . . .	Dimotus
Health. (Refer to Business, Expect, Medicine, Progress.)	
Amputation is considered necessary . .	Dionysia
Amputation is considered unnecessary . .	Diota
Attack is considered serious . .	Diphris
Attack is considered not serious . .	Diploma
Attack is considered trifling . .	Dipsacon
Has *changed* for the worse, but doctor gives hope	Dipsas

Has *changed* for the worse and doctor gives no hope	Diradio
Has *changed* for the worse and doctor gives no hope, come quickly	Directio
Has *changed* for the worse and doctor gives no hope, useless your coming . .	Direxi
Condition has changed slightly for better .	Discoquo
Condition is unchanged	Discretus
A *consulting physician* has been called in .	Discurro
A *consulting physician* is not required . .	Dispando
Continues to improve	Dispar
Is able to attend to *correspondence* . .	Dispenso
Is unable to attend to *correspondence* . .	Displodo
Doctor considers the crisis safely over . .	Dispudet
Doctor has ordered solid food . . .	Disquiro
Doctor is more hopeful to-day . . .	Dissero
Doctor states the illness to be — . .	Dissideo
Consult your *doctor*	Dissocio
Consult your *doctor* and let me know result .	Dissono
Have consulted *doctor* and he considers — .	Distraxi
Have consulted *doctor*, will post you particulars	Ditesco
Fever is increasing	Diva
Fever is subsiding	Divarico
Is able to *go out* for a drive . . .	Diverse
Is unable to *go out* for a drive . . .	Divisio
Is able to *go out* for a walk . . .	Diurnus
Is unable to *go out* for a walk . . .	Docilis
Illness commenced on the — . . .	Docte
The *improvement* is sustained . . .	Doctrina
The *improvement* is not sustained . .	Dogma
Invalid better ; doctor recommends change of air	Dolatus
Invalid is now out of danger . . .	Dolenter
Invalid is now quite well	Dolium

Invalid is now quite well and will write you	Domator
Invalid recommended change of air by doctor, and as soon as convalescent will go to —	Domitrix
Invalid the same, doctor recommends change of air	Domo
Is able to undertake the *journey* . . .	Donarium
Is unable to undertake the *journey* . .	Donax
Can take no *nourishment*	Dormisco
Can take no *nourishment,* come if possible .	Drapeta
Operation has been performed successfully .	Draucus
Operation has been performed without success	Dryades
Patient has become unconscious . . .	Dubito
Patient is now quite conscious . . .	Ducatus
Patient is still unconscious . . .	Ducenti
Is able to be *removed* from bed . . .	Duellum
Is unable to be *removed* from bed . .	Dulcedo
Is able to be *removed* to another room . .	Dulcifera
Is unable to be *removed* to another room .	Dummodo
Passed a *sleepless* night, and is feverish this morning	Duodecim
Slept well, and has taken nourishment this morning	Duplex
Is rapidly regaining *strength* . . .	Duplico
Symptoms are not considered alarming. .	Duramen
Symptoms show great improvement . .	Dureta
Symptoms show no improvement. . .	Durities
Taken ill	Dysuria
Taken ill, cannot come	Fabacia
Taken ill, cannot come to-day . .	Fabarius
Taken ill, cannot come this week. . .	Fabrica
Taken ill, cannot keep appointment . .	Fabrilis
Taken ill, cannot leave	Fabularis
Taken ill slightly, do not be alarmed . .	Fabulose
Taken ill slightly, letter by post. . .	Facesso
Taken ill slightly, no necessity for doctor .	Facetus

Taken ill slightly, no necessity for doctor, will write	**Facilis**
Taken ill slightly, will telegraph again .	**Facticius**
Taken ill slightly, will telegraph again if no better	**Factito**
Taken ill slightly, will telegraph again if worse	**Facula**
Taken ill slightly, unable to travel to-day .	**Facultas**
Taken ill slightly, unable to see you to-day	**Fageus**
Taken ill suddenly	**Fagineus**
Taken ill suddenly, come at once . .	**Falarica**
Taken ill suddenly, send doctor immediately.	**Falcifer**
Taken ill suddenly, send doctor and come yourself	**Falco**
Taken ill suddenly, and dangerously . .	**Falere**
Taken ill suddenly, and dangerously, come at once	**Falernum**
Taken ill with fever	**Faliscus**
Taken ill with fever, do not come . .	**Fallacia**
Taken ill with fever, let children remain .	**Fallax**
Telegraph health of —	**Falsus**
Telegraph health of *Baby* . . .	**Famiger**
Telegraph health of *Baby*, shall I come .	**Famosus**
Telegraph health of *Brother* . . .	**Famulor**
Telegraph health of *Brother*, shall I come .	**Fandus**
Telegraph health of *Children* . . .	**Fanum**
Telegraph health of *Children*, shall I come .	**Farcimen**
Telegraph health of *Daughter* . . .	**Farcio**
Telegraph health of *Daughter*, shall I come	**Farctura**
Telegraph health of *Father* . . .	**Farnus**
Telegraph health of *Father*, shall I come .	**Farrago**
Telegraph health of *Grandfather* . .	**Fartilis**
Telegraph health of *Grandfather*, shall I come	**Fascino**

D

Telegraph health of *Grandmother* . .	**Fasciola**
Telegraph health of *Grandmother*, shall I come	**Fastigo**
Telegraph health of *Husband* . . .	**Fastosus**
Telegraph health of *Husband*, shall I come .	**Fatifer**
Telegraph health of *invalid* . . .	**Fatisco**
Telegraph health of *Mother* . . .	**Fatuitas**
Telegraph health of *Mother*, shall I come .	**Fatum**
Telegraph health of *Sister*	**Favere**
Telegraph health of *Sister*, shall I come .	**Favilla**
Telegraph health of *Son*	**Februa**
Telegraph health of *Son*, shall I come . .	**Fecialis**
Telegraph health of *Wife*	**Fecundo**
Telegraph health of *Wife*, shall I come .	**Felineus**
Telegraph health of *yourself* . . .	**Félix**
Telegraph health of *yourself*, shall I come .	**Fellator**
Telegraph health of *yourself*, am very anxious	**Femella**
Very much better	**Femur**
Very much better, do not come, will write .	**Fenebris**
Very much better, and improving fast .	**Fenero**
Very much better, and improving fast, do . not come	**Fenestra**
Wound is healing rapidly	**Feralia**
Wound is healing satisfactorily . . .	**Fereola**
Wound is not healing satisfactorily . .	**Feretrum**
Wound is not healing very rapidly . .	**Ferio**
Please *write* fully present condition of patient	**Ferme**
(High) How *high* can I go	**Fermento**
How *high* can you go	**Ferocia**
It is too *high*	**Ferox**
Hire if possible	**Ferreus**
Hire a conveyance to meet me at — . .	**Ferrugo**

Can you *hire*	Ferrum
Do not *hire*	Fervesco

Home by first train in morning . . .	Fervidus
Home by last train to-night . . .	Ferula
Home by first train on — . . .	Fervor
Shall not be *home* this evening . .	Festiva
Shall not be *home* this evening until — .	Festuca

Hotels. (Refer to FORGET, FORWARD, LUGGAGE.)

Shall *arrive* about — o'clock . . .	Fiber
Shall *arrive* by the mail train . . .	Fibra
Shall *arrive* by the steamer due on —. .	Fibratus
Shall *arrive* by the train due at — .	Ficedula
Reserve a *single bedroom* for me to-night .	Ficetum
Reserve comfortable *single bedroom* for me to-night	Ficosus
Reserve a *single bedroom* for me to-night, shall arrive at —	Fictilis
Reserve comfortable *single bedroom* for me to-night, shall arrive at — . . .	Fictio
Reserve a *single bedroom* for me to-night, shall require —	Ficulus
Reserve comfortable *single bedroom* for me to-night, shall require — . . .	Fidenter
Reserve a *single bedroom* for me to-morrow .	Fidicen
Reserve a comfortable *single bedroom* for me to-morrow	Fidicula
Reserve a *single bedroom* for me to-morrow, shall arrive at —.	Fiducia
Reserve a comfortable *single bedroom* for me to-morrow, shall arrive at —. . .	Figlinus
Reserve a *single bedroom* for me, arriving on —	Figulina

D 2

Reserve a comfortable *single bedroom* for me, arriving on —	**Filatim**
Reserve a *double bedroom* for me for to-night	**Filictum**
Reserve a *double bedroom* for me, not too high up, for to-night	**Filiola**
Reserve a *double bedroom* for me on — .	**Filiolus**
Reserve a *double bedroom* for me, not too high up, on —	**Filius**
Reserve a *double-bedded room* for to-night .	**Filum**
Reserve a *double-bedded room*, not too high up, for to-night	**Fimbria**
Reserve a *double-bedded room* for — . .	**Finitio**
Reserve a *double-bedded room*, not too high up, for —	**Firmamen**
Reserve a *single bedroom* and sitting-room to-night, shall arrive — . . .	**Firmitas**
Reserve a *single bedroom* and sitting-room to-night, shall arrive at — . . .	**Firmus**
Reserve a *single bedroom* and sitting-room to-night, shall require — . . .	**Fiscina**
Reserve a *single bedroom* and sitting-room to-morrow	**Fissilis**
. Reserve a *double bedroom* and sitting-room to-night, shall arrive at — . . .	**Fissio**
Reserve a *double bedroom* and sitting-room to-night, shall require — . . .	**Fissura**
Reserve a *double bedroom* and sitting-room to-morrow	**Fistula**
Reserve two *single bedrooms* for to-night, shall arrive at —	**Flabilis**
Reserve two *double bedrooms* for to-night, shall arrive at —	**Flabrum**
Reserve two *double-bedded rooms* for to-night, shall arrive at — . . .	**Flaccida**
Reserve a *single bedroom* and a *double bedroom* for to-night, shall arrive at — .	**Flaccus**

Reserve a *double bedroom* and a *double-bedded room* for to-night, shall arrive at — . . . . **Flagello**

Reserve two *single bedrooms* for — . . . . **Flagito**

Reserve two *double bedrooms* for — . . . . **Flagro**

Reserve two *double-bedded rooms* for — . . . . **Flagrum**

Reserve a *single bedroom* and a *double bedroom* for — . . . . . . **Flamen**

Reserve a *single bedroom* and a *double-bedded room* for — . . . . . . **Flamma**

Reserve a *double bedroom* and a *double-bedded room* for — . . . . **Flammeus**

Reserve two *single bedrooms* and a sitting-room to-night, shall arrive at — . . **Flammula**

Reserve two *double bedrooms* and a sitting-room to-night, shall arrive at — . . **Flatus**

Reserve two *double-bedded rooms* and a sitting-room to-night, shall arrive at — **Flaveo**

Reserve a *single bedroom*, a *double bedroom*, and a sitting-room for to-night, shall arrive at — . . . . . . **Flavesco**

Reserve a *single bedroom*, a *double-bedded room*, and a sitting-room for to-night, shall arrive at — . . . . **Flecto**

Reserve a *double bedroom*, a *double-bedded room*, and a sitting-room for to-night, shall arrive at — . . . . **Fletifer**

Reserve two *single bedrooms* and a sitting-room for — . . . . . **Flexuose**

Reserve two *double bedrooms* and a sitting-room for — . . . . **Flexuosus**

Reserve two *double-bedded rooms* and a sitting-room for — . . . **Flexura**

Reserve a *single bedroom*, a *double bedroom*, and a sitting-room for — . . . **Flictus**

Reserve a *single bedroom*, a *double-bedded room*, and a sitting-room for — . . **Fligo**

Reserve a *double bedroom*, a *double-bedded room*, and a sitting-room for — . . Floralis

Reserve three *single bedrooms*, shall arrive on— Floreus

Reserve three *double bedrooms*, shall arrive on — . . . . . . Floridus

Reserve three *double-bedded rooms*, shall arrive on —. . . . . . Florifer

Reserve one *single bedroom* and two *double bedrooms*, shall arrive on — . . . Fluctus

Reserve one *single bedroom*, one *double bedroom*, and one *double-bedded room*, shall arrive on —. . . . . . Fluentum

Reserve one *single bedroom* and two *double-bedded rooms*, shall arrive on — . . Fluta

Reserve two *double bedrooms* and one *double-bedded room*, shall arrive on — . . Fluvidus

Reserve one *double bedroom* and two *double-bedded rooms*, shall arrive on — . . Fluxio

Reserve three *single bedrooms* and a sitting-room, shall arrive on — . . . Focale

Reserve three *double bedrooms* and a sitting-room, shall arrive on — . . . Focaneus

Reserve three *double-bedded rooms* and a sitting-room, shall arrive on — . . Focillo

Reserve one *single bedroom*, two *double bedrooms*, and a sitting-room, shall arrive on — Fodico

Reserve one *single bedroom*, one *double bedroom*, one *double-bedded room*, and a sitting-room, shall arrive on — . . Foliosus

Reserve one *single bedroom*, two *double-bedded rooms*, and a sitting-room, shall arrive on —. . . . . . Folium

Reserve two *double bedrooms*, one *double-bedded room*, and a sitting-room, shall arrive on —. . . . . . Follitim

Reserve one *double bedroom*, two *double-bedded rooms*, and a sitting-room, shall arrive on —	**Fomenta**
Reserve also one *maid-servants' bedroom* .	**Forabilis**
Reserve also two *maid-servants' bedrooms* .	**Foramen**
Reserve also one *man-servants' bedroom* .	**Forceps**
Reserve also two *men-servants' bedrooms* .	**Forem**
Reserve *beds* for two gentlemen to-night .	**Forensis**
Reserve *beds* for three gentlemen to-night .	**Forfex**
Reserve *beds* for four gentlemen to-night .	**Forica**
Reserve *beds* for two gentlemen to-morrow .	**Igneus**
Reserve *beds* for three gentlemen to-morrow .	**Ignigena**
Reserve *beds* for four gentlemen to-morrow .	**Ignipes**
Reserve *beds* for two gentlemen for — .	**Ignoro**
Reserve *beds* for three gentlemen for — .	**Ilex**
Reserve *beds* for four gentlemen for — .	**Ilicit**
Have a *carriage* with single horse ready for me at — o'clock	**Ilicitum**
Have a *carriage* with single horse at the station to meet train arriving — . .	**Iligneus**
Have a *carriage* with two horses ready for me at — o'clock	**Iliosus**
Have a *carriage* with two horses at the station to meet train arriving — . .	**Illabor**
Have a *fly* ready for me at — o'clock . .	**Illac**
Have a *fly* at the station to meet train arriving —	**Illaqueo**
Have an *omnibus* at the station to meet train arriving —	**Illapsa**
Have *dinner* ready this evening punctually at — o'clock	**Illatro**
Require *dinner* this evening in private room, for — persons	**Illicio**
Reserve seats at the Table d'hôte *dinner* for — persons	**Illitus**

Have a *fire* in the bedroom	Illuceo
Have *fires* in the bedroom and sitting-room .	Illumino
— *found* and forwarded as instructed . .	Imaginor
What *Hotel* do you recommend in — . .	Imago
— when did he *leave* your Hotel . .	Imberbis
— *left* in Hotel, send to me at — . .	Imbibo
— *left* in Hotel, send to me here . .	Imbrex
— *left* in my room, send to me at — .	Imbrifer
— *left* in my room, send to me here .	Imbuo
— *left* this Hotel on the — . . .	Imitamen
— *left* this Hotel to go to — . . .	Imitatio
— has not yet *left* this Hotel . . .	Immadeo
Have sent articles *left* in your room as in-structed	Immemor
Send articles *left* in my room to — . .	Immensus
Send articles *left* in my room to this address	Immergo
Have sent luggage *left* in your room, as in-structed	Immigro
Send luggage *left* in my room to — . .	Imminuo
Send luggage *left* in my room to this address	Immisceo
Any *letters* or other communication arriving for me send to —	Immixtus
Any *letters* or *telegrams* arriving for me keep until I arrive	Immodice
Any *letters* or *telegrams* arriving for me re-direct them to—	Immolo
Any *letters* or *telegrams* arriving for me re-direct them to this address . . .	Immorior
Some *letters* lying here for you, what shall be done with them	Immotus
Some *letters* and *telegrams* lying here for you, what shall be done with them .	Immugio
Some *telegrams* lying here for you, what shall be done with them	Impages
— *missing* on arrival here, can you trace it	Impasco

— *missing* on arrival, can you trace it ? if so forward to me —	Impavide
— *missing* on arrival here, have search made for it and telegraph me result . .	Impendeo
Can find no trace of the *missing* articles .	Impensus
Rooms reserved as requested . .	Imperium
Rooms reserved as requested and your orders will be attended to	Impete
Cannot reserve the *rooms* asked for. Already full	Impetigo
Please keep my *rooms ;* cannot arrive until —	Impexus
Shall not require *rooms* ordered . . .	Impietas
Shall require *supper* on arrival . . .	Impiger
If you have not already done so. . . .	Impilia
If you have not already done so, do not send	Impingo
If you have not already done so, send at once	Impius

Illness.　(Refer to HEALTH.)

(Include)—Does it *include* —	Implecto
It does not *include* —	Imploro
Were *included* in estimates . . .	Implumbo
Were not *included* in estimates . . .	Implumis
Are the terms *inclusive*	Impluo
Terms are *inclusive*	Impolitus
Terms are not *inclusive*	Impono

(Inconvenience)—Can it be done without *inconvenience*	Impos
It can be done without *inconvenience* . .	Impositio

(Inform)—Can you *inform* me . . .	Imprecor
Information has been received . . .	Imprimis
From what source is the *information* . .	Improbe
More *information* is necessary . . .	Impropero

No *information* has been received . .	Impuber
This is for your private *information* . .	Impugno
Have you *informed* —	Impulsio

Inquire. (See ENQUIRE.)

Insurance has been effected	Impunis
Insure immediately	Imulus
Cannot *insure* under —	Inambulo

(Interfere)—Decline to *interfere* . . .	Inanimus
Will not *interfere*	Inanio

Interview will be necessary	Inaniter
Interview will not be necessary . .	Inaratus

(Introduce)—Can you *introduce* me to — .	Inaresco
Introductions are sent by post . .	Inaudax

Investigate into the matter immediately . .	Inauguro
Result of *investigations* not satisfactory .	Incanto
Result of *investigations* satisfactory . .	Incassum

Invitations. (Refer to DINNER ENGAGEMENTS,
LUNCH ENGAGEMENTS, THEATRE.)

Accept your invitation with pleasure . .	Incautus
Regret I cannot *accept* your invitation .	Incedo
Shall I *accept* the invitation for — .	Incensus
Shall you *accept* the invitation for — .	Inceptor
Bring with you to-day your friend . .	Incilis
Bring your brother with you . .	Incipio
Bring your daughter with you . .	Incisura
Bring your father with you . .	Incitate
Bring your husband with you . .	Inclinis
Bring your mother with you . .	Includo
Bring your sister with you . .	Inclytus

Bring your son with you	Incoctus
Bring your wife with you	Incogito
Received invitation for —	Incoquo
Received invitation, shall I accept it, for —	Increbro
Received invitation to party to-night, at —.	Incrusto
Received invitation to party to-night. Can you come to —	Incubito
Reply, accepting the invitation . . .	Incubo
Reply, declining the invitation . . .	Incumbo
Has not *replied* to the invitation. . .	Incursio
Have not yet *replied* to the invitation. .	Incurvus
If you can arrange to *stay* to-night we can give you a bed	Indemnis
Shall be very glad if you can come and *stay* with us to-night	Indeptus
Shall be very glad if you can come and *stay* with us until —	Indicium
When can you come and *stay* with us for a few days	Indidem
Invoices have arrived	Indigena
Invoices have not arrived	Indigne
Invoices will be sent on —. . . .	Indoles
It is so	Indormio
It is not so	Inductio
It will do in default of better . . .	Inducula
It will do quite well	Indulgeo
It will not do	Indusium
(Judge)—You can best *judge* on the spot. .	Indutus
Keep possession until you hear from — .	Induxi
Will not *keep* it longer than — . . .	Inemptus
Know nothing whatever of the matter . . .	Ineptia

Known, and in good position . . .	Inequito
Is not *known* here	Inertia

Leave all matters in your hands . . .	Infabre
Leave everything just as it is . . .	Infacete
Leave has been given	Infamis
Leave has been refused	Infandus
Leave immediately on receipt of this . .	Infantia
Cannot *leave* here at present . . .	Infarcio

Leaving.   (Refer to DEPARTURE.)

Leaving on the 1st by the Steamship — .	Infatuo
Leaving on the 2nd by the Steamship — .	Infector
Leaving on the 3rd by the Steamship — .	Infelix
Leaving on the 4th by the Steamship — .	Inferveo
Leaving on the 5th by the Steamship — .	Infestus
Leaving on the 6th by the Steamship — .	Infibulo
Leaving on the 7th by the Steamship — .	Infindo
Leaving on the 8th by the Steamship — .	Infirmo
Leaving on the 9th by the Steamship — .	Inflammo
Leaving on the 10th by the Steamship — .	Inflatus
Leaving on the 11th by the Steamship — .	Inflexio
Leaving on the 12th by the Steamship — .	Infloreo
Leaving on the 13th by the Steamship — .	Informis
Leaving on the 14th by the Steamship — .	Infossus
Leaving on the 15th by the Steamship — .	Infra
Leaving on the 16th by the Steamship — .	Infundo
Leaving on the 17th by the Steamship — .	Infusio
Leaving on the 18th by the Steamship — .	Ingemino
Leaving on the 19th by the Steamship — .	Ingemo
Leaving on the 20th by the Steamship — .	Ingenium
Leaving on the 21st by the Steamship — .	Ingenue
Leaving on the 22nd by the Steamship — .	Ingestum
Leaving on the 23rd by the Steamship — .	Ingrate
Leaving on the 24th by the Steamship — .	Ingravo
Leaving on the 25th by the Steamship — .	Ingressio

Leaving on the 26th by the Steamship — .	Ingruo
Leaving on the 27th by the Steamship — .	Inhabito
Leaving on the 28th by the Steamship — .	Inhorreo
Leaving on the 29th by the Steamship — .	Inhumo
Leaving on the 30th by the Steamship — .	Inimico
Leaving on the 31st by the Steamship — .	Inique

Legal. (Refer to POSTPONE, POWER.)

Appeal has been allowed, costs in the cause .	Initio
Appeal has been allowed, with costs . .	Injectio
Appeal has been dismissed, costs in the cause	Injungo
Appeal has been dismissed, with costs . .	Injura
Attorney for the defendant is — . . .	Injussus
Attorney for the plaintiff is — . . .	Injuste
Attorney on the other side is — . . .	Innato
Who is the *attorney* for —	Innitor
Who is the *attorney* for the defendant .	Innocens
Who is the *attorney* for the plaintiff . .	Innovo
Who is the *attorney* on the other side . .	Innoxius
Bail has been accepted	Innuptus
Bail has been refused	Innutrio
Bail is required for —	Inocco
Counsel for the *defendant* has commenced his cross-examination	Inoculo
Counsel for the defendant has finished his cross-examination	Inodorus
Counsel for the defendant has commenced his speech	Inopaco
Counsel for the defendant has finished his speech	Inopinus
Counsel for the defendant has commenced calling his witnesses	Inoratus
Counsel for the defendant has finished calling his witnesses	Inornate
Counsel for the *plaintiff* has commenced his cross-examination	Inquam

Counsel for the plaintiff has finished his cross-examination	Inquiro
Counsel for the plaintiff has commenced his speech	Insanio
Counsel for the plaintiff has finished his speech	Inscendo
Counsel for the plaintiff has commenced calling his witnesses	Insciens
Counsel for the plaintiff has finished calling his witnesses	Inscribo
Opinion of counsel is against them . .	Insculpo
Opinion of *counsel* is against us . . .	Inseco
Opinion of *counsel* is against you . .	Insequor
Opinion of *counsel* is in our favour . .	Insertim
Opinion of *counsel* is in their favour . .	Inservio
Opinion of *counsel* is in your favour . .	Insidior
Retain as *counsel* on my behalf — . .	Insido
Defendant has retained as his *counsel* — .	Insignis
Have retained as *counsel* on your behalf — .	Insimulo
Plaintiff has retained as his *counsel* — .	Insisto
Case is in the list for *hearing* to-morrow .	Insolens
Case is not in the list for *hearing* to-morrow	Insolida
When will the case be in the list for *hearing*	Inspergo
Hearing of the case commenced to-day, adjourned until —	Inspicio
Hearing of the case commenced to-day, adjourned until to-morrow . . .	Insterno
Hearing of the case concluded, judgment reserved	Instillo
Hearing of the case concluded, jury have retired	Instruo
Hearing of the case will be concluded to-day	Insuasum
Hearing of the case will be concluded to-morrow	Insula

Hearing of the case will be concluded this week	**Insurgo**
Hearing of the case will last for several days	**Intectus**
Judge has commenced his summing-up .	**Integro**
Judge has concluded his summing-up . .	**Maceria**
Judge has concluded his summing-up. It was in favour of defendant . . .	**Macies**
Judge has concluded his summing-up. It was in favour of neither party . .	**Mactator**
Judge has concluded his summing-up. It was in favour of plaintiff . . .	**Madefeci**
Jury are still absent	**Madulsa**
Jury could not agree, and have been discharged	**Magnus**
Subpœna as a witness on our side — . .	**Majestas**
Subpœna has been served on — . . .	**Malache**
Subpœna has not been served, as we cannot find —	**Maledice**
Summons has been issued, returnable on —	**Maligne**
Summons heard to-day. Adjourned for a week	**Manceps**
Summons heard to-day. Adjourned into court	**Manedum**
Summons heard to-day. Adjourned until —	**Manesis**
Summons heard to-day. Chief clerk reserves decision	**Manifeste**
Summons heard to-day. Master reserves decision	**Manliana**
Summons heard to-day. Order made as asked	**Mansito**
Summons heard to-day. Order refused .	**Mansuete**
Summons heard to-day. Order refused, with costs	**Marceo**

Summons heard to-day. Referred to judge in chambers	Margaris
Verdict against us	Margino
Verdict for —	Marinus
Verdict for the defendant, with costs . .	Masculus
Verdict for the defendant, without costs .	Maspetum
Verdict for the plaintiff, damages — .	Mastigia
Verdict for the plaintiff, with costs .	Mastruca
Verdict for the plaintiff, without costs .	Matellio
Verdict in our favour	Mater
Verdict of guilty. Sentence — .	Maternus
Verdict of guilty. Sentence deferred .	Matralia
Verdict of manslaughter. Sentence —	Matrimus
Verdict of manslaughter. Sentence deferred	Mature
Verdict of not guilty	Maxilla
Verdict of not proven	Maxime
Verdict of temporary insanity . .	Meatus
Verdict of wilful murder . . .	Mecastor
Witnesses must be in attendance on — .	Meconis
Your attendance in court as *witness* is required —	Medianus
Writ has been issued as requested . .	Medicina
Writ has been served on all the defendants .	Medicus
Writ has been served on the defendant .	Meditor
Writ has not yet been served on the defendant	Medium
Have obtained order for substituted service of *writ*	Megalium
Length is —	Melampus
What is the *length* of — . . .	Melania
Let on the terms agreed the — . . .	Melitites
Let on the terms named the — . .	Mellifer

Letter. (Refer to Acknowledge, Expecting, Forward, Hotels, Post, Reply, Wait, Writing, Wrote.)

Letter last received was dated — . .	**Melligo**
Been obliged to leave before the arrival of your *letter*. Telegraph to — . .	**Mellilla**
Been obliged to leave before the arrival of your *letter*. Write again to — . .	**Mellinia**
Do not forward any more *letters*. Keep them until my return	**Mellis**
Forward all *letters* until further instructions to —	**Mellitorum**
Forward my *letters* to-day to Poste Restante —	**Mellitum**
Forward my *letters* to-day and to-morrow to Poste Restante —	**Mello**
Forward my *letters* until further instructions to Poste Restante —	**Mellorum**
Forward my *letters* to-day to Poste Restante here	**Mellum**
Forward my *letters* to-day and to-morrow to Poste Restante here	**Melofolia**
Forward my *letters* until further instructions to Poste Restante here	**Melofoliam**
Forward my *letters* to —	**Melomeli**
Have received *letter* from — . . .	**Melopepo**
Have not received *letter* from — . .	**Membrana**
Have not received your *letter* . .	**Memento**
Have not received any *letter* from you since —	**Meminisse**
Have not received any *letter* from you. Telegraph at once to — . . .	**Memoris**
Have not received any *letter* from you. Write at once to —	**Memoratus**
Have you received my *letter* . . .	**Memoro**
Have you received my *letter* with enclosures	**Mendacis**

E

Have you received my *letter;* no reply received, telegraph	Mendose
Private *letter* posted you to-day . .	Mensio
Private *letter* posted to-day to — . .	Mensula
Private *letter* posted you yesterday . .	Mentagra
Private *letter* posted yesterday to — . .	Mentum
Private *letter* not received	Mercator
Private *letter* received	Merenda
Received your *letter*	Mergo
Received your *letter* and enclosures . .	Meridies
Received your *letter* and forwarded it as requested	Merulam
Received your *letter,* and instructions noted	Mespilum
Received your *letter* and returned it to you .	Metallum
Received your *letter* and telegram . .	Metaphora
Received your *letter* and telegram ; having attention	Metatio
Received your *letter* and will attend to it immediately	Metopion
Received your *letter* and will attend to it as soon as possible	Metreta
Received your *letter;* attending to contents	Metuo
Received your *letter;* attended to contents and writing	Migratio
Received your *letter,* but no enclosures .	Militia
Received your *letter;* cannot do as you wish	Milvago
Received your *letter;* cannot reply until —	Milvinus
Received your *letter* containing cheque .	Minister
Received your *letter* containing P.O.O. .	Minium
Received your *letter;* do not understand — .	Minor
Received your *letter;* do not understand first portion	Minutal
Received your *letter ;* do not understand latter portion	Mirmillo
Received your *letter ;* have already sent .	Miseria
Received your *letter ;* have replied fully .	Mithrax

Received your *letter;* order will be attended to	Mitra
Received your *letter;* orders will be attended to at once	Mixtim
Received your *letter;* too busy to attend to matter	Mixtura
Received your *letter;* too unwell to write .	Mobilior
Received your *letter;* too unwell to attend to matter	Modestia
Received your *letter;* will do as you wish .	Modius
Received your *letter;* will post you particulars of —	Modulate
What is the date of the last *letter* . .	Molimen

(Litigation)—Do your utmost to avoid *litigation*	Molitura

Lodgings. (Refer to APARTMENTS.)

Lose no time in the matter . . .	Mollesca
Do not *lose* an instant . . .	Momentum
Do not *lose* an instant, but come at once .	Monedula

Loss. (Refer to FORGET, HOTELS.)

Luggage. (Refer to FORGET, FORWARD, HOTELS.)

Luggage has been left behind; enquire at the station	Monitor
Leave your *luggage* at the cloakroom to be called for. . . .	Monstro
Send my *luggage* on to — . . .	Montuosus
Send a conveyance to take the *luggage* .	Moralis
Will send a man to take charge of the *luggage*	Morbidus

Lunch. (Refer to INVITATIONS.)

Will *lunch* with you — . . .	Morbonia

E 2

Will *lunch* with you to-day . . .	**Mordax**
Will *lunch* with you to-day, and wait your arrival at —	**Morigero**
Will *lunch* with you to-day, and will call at —	**Mormyr**
Will *lunch* with you to-morrow . . .	**Morose**
Will *lunch* with you to-morrow, and wait your arrival	**Morpheus**
Will *lunch* with you and call at — . .	**Motus**
Will *lunch* with you on Monday . .	**Mucidus**
Will *lunch* with you on Tuesday . .	**Muginor**
Will *lunch* with you on Wednesday . .	**Mugitus**
Will *lunch* with you on Thursday . .	**Mulctrum**
Will *lunch* with you on Friday . . .	**Multifer**
Will *lunch* with you on Saturday . .	**Munditer**
Will *lunch* with you on Sunday . . .	**Municeps**
Will you *lunch* with me — . . .	**Munifice**
Will you *lunch* with me to-day at — . .	**Murcidus**
Will you *lunch* with me to-day at the Club at —	**Muraena**
Will you *lunch* with me here at — . .	**Musca**
Will you *lunch* with me to-day; will call for you at —	**Muscosus**
Will you *lunch* with me to-day; call for me at —	**Museus**
Will you *lunch* with me to-morrow at — .	**Mussito**
Will you *lunch* with me to-morrow at the Club	**Mustace**
Will you *lunch* with me to-morrow here at —	**Mutatio**
Will you *lunch* with me to-morrow; will call for you at —	**Myiagros**
Will you *lunch* with me to-morrow; call for me at —	**Myoparo**
Will you *lunch* with me on Monday at — .	**Myrapium**
Will you *lunch* with me on Tuesday at — .	**Myropola**
Will you *lunch* with me on Wednesday at—	**Myrrha**

Will you *lunch* with me on Thursday at   .   Myscus
Will you *lunch* with me on Friday at —   .   Myxa
Will you *lunch* with me on Saturday at — .   Nablium
Will you *lunch* with me on Sunday at —   .   Nactus

Machine has arrived   .   .   .   .   Nanus
Machine has arrived, and works well   .   Nape
Machine has arrived, but works badly.   .   Naphtha
Machinery out of order, delay will be great .   Napina

Many happy returns of the day   .   .   Nardinus
How *many* did you send   .   .   .   Nardum
How *many* do you want   .   .   .   Narrator

Market fully supplied .   .   .   .   Narratus
Market fully supplied, prospects bad   .   Narro
Market glutted, prospects very bad   .   Narthex
Market very flat   .   .   .   .   Nascor

Marriage has been arranged between — .   .   Nasum
Marriage is announced of —   .   .   Nasutus
Marriage postponed in consequence of —   .   Natalis
Marriage postponed indefinitely .   .   Natatio
Marriage postponed, particulars by letter .   Natator
Marriage postponed until —   .   .   Nativus
Marriage takes place at —.   .   .   Natta
Marriage takes place on —.   .   .   Naulium
Marriage takes place on Monday.   .   Nauplius
Marriage takes place on Tuesday.   .   Nausea
Marriage takes place on Wednesday   .   Nauseola
Marriage takes place on Thursday   .   Nauticus
Marriage takes place on Friday .   .   Naviger
Marriage takes place on Saturday   .   Navigium
Marriage takes place on Sunday.   .   Navigo
Marriage takes place January   .   .   Navorum
Marriage takes place February   .   .   Nebritis

Marriage takes place March	.	.	.	Necesse
Marriage takes place April.	.	.	.	Necessum
Marriage takes place May .	.	.	.	Necnon
Marriage takes place June .	.	.	.	Nectarea
Marriage takes place July .	.	.	.	Necubi
Marriage takes place August	.	.	.	Necunde
Marriage takes place September .	.	.	Nefandus
Marriage takes place October	.	.	.	Nefarie
Marriage takes place November .	.	.	Nefarius
Marriage takes place December .	.	.	Nefas
Marriage will not take place	.	.	.	Nefastus
Marriage will not take place; particulars by letter				Negantia
Married to-day .	.	.	.	Negatio
Married yesterday·	.	.	.	Negito

Medicine not arrived ·	.	.	.	Negligo
Medicine not arrived, send at once	.	.	Negotium
Medicine wanted immediately	.	.	Nepeta

Meet. (Refer to Appointments.)

Meet me at — .	.	.	.	Nepos
Meet me at 1 o'clock at —.	.	.	Neptis
Meet me at 1.30 at —	.	.	.	Nequam
Meet me at 2 at — .	.	.	.	Neque
Meet me at 2.30 at —	.	.	.	Nequid
Meet me at 3 at — .	.	.	.	Nequities
Meet me at 3.30 at —	.	.	.	Nervose
Meet me at 4 at — .	.	.	.	Nervosus
Meet me at 4.30 at —	.	.	.	Nervulus
Meet me at 5 at — .	.	.	.	Nescio
Meet me at 5.30 at —	.	.	.	Nescius
Meet me at 6 at — .	.	.	.	Neuradis
Meet me at 6.30 at —	.	.	.	Neuricus
Meet me at 7 at — .	.	.	.	Neutro
Meet me at 7.30 at —	.	.	.	Nexilis

Meet me at 8 at —	**Nexum**
Meet me at 8.30 at —	**Nictatio**
Meet me at 9 at —	**Nicto**
Meet me at 9.30 at —	**Nidorem**
Meet me at 10 at —	**Nidulor**
Meet me at 10.30 at —	**Nidulus**
Meet me at 11 at —	**Nigellus**
Meet me at 11.30 at —	**Nigra**
Meet me at 12 at —	**Nigrina**
Meet me at 12.30 at —	**Nigresco**
Meet me on Monday at —. . . .	**Nigro**
Meet me on Tuesday at —. . . .	**Nihil**
Meet me on Wednesday at — . .	**Nihildum**
Meet me on Thursday at — . .	**Nilios**
Meet me on Friday at — . . .	**Nilum**
Meet me on Saturday at — . .	**Nimbifer**
Meet me on Sunday at — . . .	**Nimbosus**
Meet me this morning at — . .	**Nimbus**
Meet me this afternoon at — . .	**Nimietas**
Meet me this evening at — . .	**Nimio**
Meet me to-night at — . . .	**Nimirum**
Meet me to-morrow morning at — .	**Niteo**
Meet me to-morrow evening — . .	**Nitescat**
Meet me to-morrow afternoon at — .	**Nitido**
Can you *meet* me at — . . .	**Nitidus**
Can you *meet* me as suggested . .	**Nitraria**
Can you *meet* me to-day . . .	**Nitratus**
Can you *meet* me this evening . .	**Nitrum**
Cannot *meet* you as arranged . .	**Nivarius**
Cannot *meet* you as arranged, will explain later	**Nivatus**
Cannot *meet* you until —	**Niveus**
Meeting postponed	**Nobilis**
Meeting postponed until — . . .	**Nobilito**
Meeting takes place on — . . .	**Nobis**
Meeting takes place to-morrow . .	**Nocenter**

Cannot attend the *meeting* of the Board .	Nocivus
Cannot attend the *meeting* of the Committee	Noctifer

Met with. (Refer to ACCIDENT.)

Military. (Refer to HEALTH.)

Consult the colonel and let me know result .	Noctua
Will you *exchange* with me . . .	Nodor
Will you *exchange* with me for — . .	Nodosus
Will you sanction *exchange* with — .	Nominito
Can my leave be *extended* to — . . .	Nomino
Extension of leave cannot be sanctioned .	Nomus
Extension of leave cannot be sanctioned, you must return at once	Nonageni
Extension of leave required . . .	Nonagies
Extension of leave required on legal affairs until —	Nonanus
Extension of leave required on urgent family affairs until —	Nonassis
Extension of leave required on urgent private affairs until —	Nondum
Extension of leave required, please sanction until —	Nonnemo
Extension of leave required until — .	Nonnihil
Extension of leave sanctioned . . .	Norma
Extension of leave sanctioned until — .	Normalis
Is my *extension* of leave sanctioned .	Noscito
Furlough to all officers on leave has been cancelled, and they are ordered to rejoin their regiments by —	Nosco
Furlough to all officers on leave has been cancelled, and they are ordered to rejoin at once	Nossem
The prohibition of *furlough* to officers on leave has been cancelled . . .	Noster
You are *gazetted*	Nostras

You are *gazetted* —	Notans
You are *gazetted* Lieutenant-Colonel . .	Notarius
You are *gazetted* Major	Notesco
You are *gazetted* Captain	Nothus
You are *gazetted* to a Company . . .	Novacula
You are *gazetted* to a Troop . . .	Novalis
— was *killed* in the engagement at — .	Novatrix
— was *killed* in the last engagement . .	Nove
Ordered home on sick leave . . .	Novello
The *Regiment* has been ordered to — . .	Noveni
The *Regiment* has been ordered to Canada .	Noverca
The *Regiment* has been ordered to Cyprus .	Novicius
The *Regiment* has been ordered to Egypt .	Novum
The *Regiment* has been ordered to England .	Noxia
The *Regiment* has been ordered to Gibraltar.	Noxiosus
The *Regiment* has been ordered to India .	Noxius
The *Regiment* has been ordered to Ireland .	Nubecula
The *Regiment* has been ordered to Malta .	Nuberum
The *Regiment* has been ordered to South Africa	Nubifer
The *Regiment* has been ordered to West Indies	Nubigena
The *Regiment* suffered little in the last engagement	Nubila
The *Regiment* suffered severely in the last engagement.	Nubilans
The *Regiment* took part in the battle at — .	Nucearum
The *Regiment* took part in the skirmish at—	Nucetum
Is *report* correct here that Regiment is ordered —	Nugator
Is *report* correct here that Regiment is ordered home	Nugax
Is *report* correct here that Regiment is ordered to Canada	Nullus
Is *report* correct here that Regiment is ordered to Cyprus	Numella

Is *report* correct here that Regiment is ordered to Egypt	Numero
Is *report* correct here that Regiment is ordered to Gibraltar	Numisma
Is *report* correct here that Regiment is ordered to India	Nummatus .
Is *report* correct here that Regiment is ordered to Ireland	Numne
Is *report* correct here that Regiment is ordered to Malta	Numquis
Is *report* correct here that Regiment is ordered to South Africa . . .	Nunccine
Is *report* correct here that Regiment is ordered to West Indies	Nuncubi
War has been declared between — . .	Nundinum
War is expected to be declared between — .	Nunquam
May I *withdraw* papers	Nunquid
You may *withdraw* papers	Nuntio
You may not *withdraw* papers . . .	Nuper
Was *wounded* severely	Nuperus
Was *wounded* slightly	Nupta
Was not *wounded* nor hurt	Nupturus

Miss the Train. (Refer to TRAIN.)

Missing. (Refer to FORGET, HOTELS, LUGGAGE.)

Mistake has been discovered and rectified. .	Nuribus
Mistake has not been made on this side .	Nutamen
Correct the *mistake* without delay . .	Nutrico
Have you discovered the *mistake*. . .	Nutrimen

Money. (Refer to ACCOUNT, CHEQUE, PLACE, REMITTANCE.)

Money is nearly exhausted. When will more be provided	Nutritus

Money is very plentiful in the market . . .	**Nutrix**
Money is very scarce in the market . . .	**Nycteris**
Money will be forthcoming when required .	**Nympha**
No *money*, cannot leave until debts paid, remit —	**Obambulo**
No *money*, in great difficulties, remit — .	**Obarmo**
No *money*, send at once £5	**Obba**
No *money*, send at once £10 . . .	**Obcalleo**
No *money*, send at once £20 . . .	**Obdormio**
No *money*, send at once £25 . . .	**Obduco**
No *money*, send at once £50 . . .	**Obductio**
No *money*, send at once £75 . . .	**Obedio**
No *money*, send at once £100 . . .	**Obeliscus**
No *money*, send at once £150 . . .	**Oberro**
No *money*, send at once £200 . . .	**Obesitas**
No *money*, send at once £250 . . .	**Obfero**
No *money*, pay passage at Agent's and telegraph	**Obgannio**
No *money*, telegraph some through —. .	**Obiratus**
No *money* to pay bills . . .	**Obitus**
No *money* to pay bills before leaving, remit—	**Objaceo**
No *money* to pay passage, remit — . .	**Objectus**
No *money* to pay passage, remit by telegraph	**Oblatro**
No *money* to pay wages, remit quickly. .	**Oblatus**
No *money*, very ill, and want to come home .	**Oblique**
Name you ask for is —	**Oblisus**
Do not know the *name* of — . . .	**Oblivio**
Send *name* of —	**Oblivium**
(Nature)—What is the *nature* of the communication from —	**Oblocutor**
Negotiations are pending	**Oblongus**
Negotiations are suspended temporarily .	**Obloquor**
Have broken off *negotiations* . .	**Obluctor**

(Net)—Is it *net*	Obmolio
It is *net*	Obmotus
· Quotation is *net*	Obmoveo
None is to be got	Obnitor
· **Note** my address at foot	Obnixe
Note my address at foot for the present .	Obnuntio
Notice must immediately be given to . .	Oboleo
Have given *notice* to — . . .	Oboritor
Have received *notice* from — . . .	Obrigeo
Number you inquire for is —. . . .	Obrodo
What is the *number* of —. . . .	Obrussa
Object very strongly	Obsaturo
Have no *objection*	Obsecro
Have you any *objection*	Obsepio
Obtain as much as possible	Obsequor
Obtained what was wanted . . .	Obsessio
Can you *obtain* —	Obsidium
It cannot be *obtained*	Obsolete
Offer is accepted	Obsono
Offer is refused	Obstipus
Offer was made too late . . .	Obstiti
Can you *offer* more on same terms .	Obsto
Cannot *offer* more	Obstrepo
Make an *offer* of —	Obstupeo
Opportunity has gone by . . .	Obsutus
Opportunity has not arisen . . .	Obtectus
Wait for a better *opportunity* . .	Obtero

Option will be given for —	Obtestor
Option will be given until — . . .	Obtorpeo
Cannot give *option*	Obtortus

Order. (Refer to CANCEL, GOODS.)

Order cannot be executed	Obtrudo
Order cannot be executed until — . .	Obtrunco
Order executed before your telegram arrived	Obumbro
Order is already executed	Obuncus
All your *orders* have been executed . .	Obvagio
Am without *orders*	Obversor
Cannot accept your *order* for — . . .	Obverto
Have received your *order*. Goods will be despatched to-day	Obvertunto
Have received your *order*. Goods will be despatched to-morrow	Obvigilat
Have received your *order*. Goods will be despatched this week	Obvigilavi
Have received your *order*. Goods will be despatched next week	Obvigilo
Have received your *order*. Goods will be despatched in — weeks . . .	Obviam
Have you executed our last *order* . .	Obvius
Is not according to *order*	Obvolvo
Reply by post when you will despatch our *order* of —	Obvolvunt
Reply by telegram when you will despatch our *order* of —	Occallatus
This *order* is in addition to previous .	Occalleo
This *order* is in substitution of previous .	Occanere
This *order* must leave you on — . .	Occano
Wait cash before executing *order* . .	Occasio
When is the earliest you can deliver *order* .	Occasiones
Will accept your *order* for — . . .	Occasus
Your *order* is being executed . . .	Occator

(**Owing**)—What is *owing* from — .   .   .   Occento
What is *owing* to — .   .   .   .   Occentus

(**Paid**)—Has been *paid* .   .   .   .   Occiduus .
Has it been *paid*   .   .   .   .   Occiput
Has not been *paid*   .   .   .   .   Occisor
Have you *paid* .   .   .   .   Occludo
Must not be *paid*   .   .   .   .   Occulco
Will be *paid*   .   .   .   .   Occurro
Will not be *paid*   .   .   .   .   Oceanus

Parcel.   (Refer to SEND.)
Parcel has been forwarded .   .   .   .   Ocellus
Parcel is waiting remittance   .   .   .   Ochra
Parcel must be forwarded by passenger
    train .   .   .   .   .   .   Ocimum
Parcel received all right   .   .   .   Ocrea
Have not received the *parcel*   .   .   Octans
Have you received the *parcel*   .   .   Octipes
How was the *parcel* forwarded .   .   .   Octogeni
When was the *parcel* forwarded .   .   .   Octuplus

Passage.   (Refer to MONEY, SHIP, WEATHER.)
Passage paid here, call for particulars and
    tickets at — .   .   .   .   Octussis
Passage paid here, telegraph departure, call
    for particulars at — .   .   .   Odeum
Take *passage* by the — .   .   .   .   Odi
Take *passage.* by the — , and telegraph
    departure .   .   .   .   .   Odiosum
Take *passage,* and come at once by the — .   Odor
Take *passage,* and come at once, telegraph
    departure .   .   .   .   .   .   Odoratio

Patterns are suitable.   .   .   .   .   Odoratus
Patterns are suitable, but material too cheap   Odyssea

Patterns are suitable, but material too dear .	Ofella
Patterns are not suitable	Offatim
Can supply that *pattern* in — . . .	Offectus
Have you more of the same *pattern* in stock	Officina
Have you much of the same *pattern* in stock	Officiose
How soon can you supply more of the same *pattern*	Officium
No more of the same *pattern* in stock . .	Offlecto
Not much of the same *pattern* in stock .	Offucia
Plenty of the same *pattern* in stock . .	Offula
Price of that *pattern* better quality is — .	Offundo
Price of that *pattern* lower quality is — .	Offusus
Price of that *pattern* same quality is — .	Oggero
Quote price of *pattern* sent in better quality	Oleaceus
Quote price of *pattern* sent in lower quality .	Oleaster
Send at once a selection of *patterns* . .	Oleitas
Pay on our account	Oleosus
Cannot *pay*	Oletum
Cannot *pay* at present	Olfactus
Do not *pay*	Olidus
Do not *pay* at present	Olitor
How do you propose to *pay* . . .	Olivetum
How much is there to *pay*	Olivina
Refuses to *pay*	Olivum
Will *pay* by instalments	Ollaris
Payment must be made against delivery . .	Olorifer
Payment must be made with order . .	Olorinus
Have sold for prompt *payment* . . .	Olus
How is *payment* to be made . . .	Olyra
Permission cannot be obtained . . .	Omasum
Permission has been obtained . . .	Ombria
I give *permission*	Omen
I will not give *permission* . . .	Omentum

Place to my account . . . . . Ominator
 Place to my account at — . . . Ominor
 Place to my account at agent's . . . Ominose
 Place to my account at Bank . . . Omitto
 Place to my account and I will repay you £— Omnifer

Plans have arrived and are approved . . Omnimodo
 Plans have not yet come to hand . . Onager
 Plans submitted will not do . . . Onagrus
 Plans will be sent for approval . . . Onero
 Errors in the *plans* will be corrected . . Onerosus
 Submit *plans* as early as possible . . Onuris

Possession will be given on the — . . . Onustus
 It is not in my *possession* . . . . Opacitas
 It is not in their *possession* . . . Opalia

Post. (Refer to LETTERS, ORDER, WRITING, WROTE.)
 Post is late to-day; letters not yet delivered Operatio
 Post in a registered letter . . . . Opertus
 Have sent by *post* . . . . . Ophidion
 Have sent by *post* in a registered letter . Ophiusa

Posted letter to-day . . . . . Opicam
 Posted letter to-day, but omitted to en-
  close — . . . . . . Opifer
 Posted letter to-day containing — . . Opimitas
 Posted letter to-day containing cheque; ac-
  knowledge receipt . . . . Opinator
 Posted letter to-day containing post office
  order; acknowledge receipt . . . Opinor
 Posted letter to-day, do not act before receipt Opipare
 Posted letter to-day, do not act on it . . Opis
 Posted letter to-day, do not act on it, another
  follows . . . . . . Opopanax

Posted letter to-day, do not leave before
   receipt .   .   .   .   .   .   Oporice
Posted letter to-day, forward to — .   . Oporteo
Posted letter to-day, keep it until — . . Oppango
Posted letter to-day, return it unopened . Oppecto
Posted letter to-day with full instructions . Oppico
Posted letter to-day with full particulars . Opploro
Posted letter to-day with necessary docu-
   ments .   .   .   .   .   .   Oppono
Posted letter yesterday   .   .   . Oppugno
Posted letter last mail   .   .   . Optimus
Posting letter by this mail   .   . Optio

Post Office order duly received   .   . Optivus
Post Office order not yet to hand   . Opulens
Have sent by *Post Office order* .   . Opulus
Send by *Post Office order* .   .   . Opuntia
Will send by *Post Office order* .   . Orarius

Poste Restante. (Refer to Letters, Telegram.)
Poste Restante .   .   .   .   . Orarum

Postpone visit, an accident has happened, letter
   by post .   .   .   .   . Oratio
Postpone visit for a few days, letter by post. Orbator
Postpone visit on account of illness . . Orbitas
Postpone visit, reasons by letter .   . Orca
Postpone visit until — .   .   . Orchis
Postpone visit until to-morrow .   . Orcula
Postpone visit until Monday   .   . Ordino
Postpone visit until Tuesday   .   . Orexis
Postpone visit until Wednesday .   . Organum
Postpone visit until Thursday .   . Origo
Postpone visit until Friday   .   . Orites
Postpone visit until Saturday   .   . Ornate
Postpone visit until Sunday   .   . Ornatrix

F

Get case *postponed* . . . . . Ornatus
Get case *postponed* until arrival of next mail   Ornithon
Get case *postponed,* important evidence by
   post . . . . Orobitis
Get case *postponed* until —. . . . Orphus

Power of Attorney must be sent to — . . Oscito
Power of Attorney sent by post . . . Osculum
Have given full *Power* to act for me to — . Ostendo
Have you sent *Power* of Attorney . . Ostensus
Impossible to act without *Power* of Attorney   Ostentum
You have full *power* to act for me . . Ostiatim

Premium asked is — . . . . Ostium
What *premium* will be payable . . . Otiose

Prevent it if possible . . . . . Ovatio

Price at present asked is — . . . . Oviaria
Cannot give the *price.* . . . . Ovillus
Send by post *price* of — . . . Ovis
What is the present *price* of — . . Ovum
What *price* will you take . . . Pabulum

(Private)—This communication is strictly *private*   Pacator

Procure as much as you can . . . Pacifico
Procure what you want on the spot . . Paciscor
Cannot be *procured* . . . . Pactilis
Can you *procure* — . . . . Palacra
Will *procure* what you want . . . Palatum

Profit will be large. . . . . Pallesco
Profit will be small . . . . Palmifer
There will be no *profit* . . . Palmula
What will be the *profit* . . . Palpamen

Progress.   (Refer to HEALTH.)

Progressing slowly but satisfactorily .	**Palpaminum**
Making good *progress* . . .	**Palpare**
Making little *progress* . . .	**Palpat**
Making no *progress* . . .	**Palpamus**
What *progress* are you making .	**Palpandum**

(Promise)—Can you not *promise* it before —	**Palpatio**
Can you *promise*	**Palpebra**
How soon can you *promise* . .	**Paluster**
Unable to *promise*	**Panchrus**

Prompt attention is required . .	**Pannosus**
Prompt delivery is essential . .	**Panther**
Reply as *promptly* as possible . .	**Papilla**

Proposal is accepted	**Parabole**
Accept the *proposal* . . .	**Paralios**
Cannot accept the *proposal* . .	**Parcitas**
Do not accept the *proposal* . .	**Parento**
Have you any *proposal* to make .	**Parocha**
Is the *proposal* accepted. . .	**Paropsis**
Proposal entertained, but modifications necessary	**Particeps**
Refuses to entertain the *proposal* .	**Parumper**
Shall be happy to entertain the *proposal* .	**Passim**
Shall I accept the *proposal* . .	**Pastinum**
Will not entertain the *proposal* . .	**Patella**
Would a *proposal* from me be entertained .	**Patesco**

Purchase for me	**Patina**
Do not *purchase* . . .	**Patrona**
For what can it be *purchased* . .	**Patruus**
What amount can you *purchase* .	**Pauci**
When will *purchase* be completed .	**Paulatim**

F 2

(Purpose)—For what *purpose* do you require   .   Pavidus

Quality must be guaranteed   .   .   .   .   Peccatus
   Is the *quality* guaranteed   .   ,   .   .   Pecco
   Quality not equal to sample   .   .   .   Pecten
   Must be of the best *quality*   .   .   .   Peculio

Quantity on hand is —   .   .   .   .   .   Pedamen
   What *quantity* can you get   .   .   .   Pedandus
   What *quantity* do you require   .   .   .   Pedes
   What *quantity* have you on hand   .   .   Pedester

(Question)—Cannot answer the *question* .   .   Pedica
   What is the *question* .   .   .   .   Pegma
   Why have you not answered my *question*   .   Pelagius

(Quick)—Be as *quick* as possible   .   .   Pelasga

Racing.
   Acceptances will be published on —   .   .   Pellitus
   — is sure to *accept*   .   .   .   .   Peltasta
   — know positively this will not *accept*   .   Peltiger
   Better be full *against* —   .   .   .   Pelvis
   Impossible to get an offer *against* — .   Penates
   — *Back* this as quickly as possible   .   Pendulus
   — *Back* this at starting price   .   .   Penniger
   — *Back* this for a place   .   .   .   Pensilis
   — *Back* this for a place, best outsider.   .   Penso
   — *Back* this for double event   .   .   Pependi
   — is *backed* for genuine money .   .   Peplus
   — is being well *backed* by —   .   .   Peragito
   — is not *backed* for genuine money   .   .   Perasper
   To what extent do you think you can *back* .   Perbelle
   — will be well *backed*   .   .   .   Perbibo
   — will probably go *back* in the betting   .   Perbonus
   Send me latest *betting*   .   .   .   .   Percaleo

Make your *book* for —	Perceptio
— has *broken down*	Percingo
— has not *broken down* as reported . .	Percoquo
— is reported to have *broken down* . .	Percrepo
— *cantered* only	Perdisco
— has done a good *canter* to-day .	Perdives
— has been *cast* in his box . . .	Perdomo
— reported to have been *cast* in his box .	Perduim
No *change* since last report. . . .	Perfecte
Send me latest *changes*	Perferus
Answer when *commission* executed . .	Perfidia
Do not execute *commission* in London .	Perflo
Execute *commission* where you please .	Perfrico
— is *coughing*	Perfundo
— is reported to be *coughing* . .	Perfusio
Cover the money laid against — . .	Pergula
is *covering* money only which is going on —	Peritus
Dead-heat. Stakes divided . . .	Perlabor
Dead-heat. Will be run off . . .	Perlate
— is *disqualified* by death of owner .	Perlonge
— is *disqualified* for —	Perlubet
Winner was *disqualified,* could not draw weight.	Permano
Winner was *disqualified* for carrying over-weight.	Permotus
Winner was *disqualified* for crossing .	Permunio
Winner was *disqualified* for foul riding .	Pernix
Do nothing until you hear from me again .	Pernocto
— is a *doubtful* runner . . .	Perpaco
Do not *fancy* —	Perparum
There will be a large *field* . . .	Perpendo
There will be a small *field* . . .	Perplexe
It is reported the *field* will be large .	Perpolio
It is reported the *field* will be small .	Perprimo
— has done a good *gallop* . . .	Perrogo
Answer if you cannot *get on* . . .	Persea

— has *gone* to —	Persisto
Am told this is a *good* thing for — .	Perspexl
— is *good*	Persuasi
Hedge quickly all you have against —.	Persulto
Hedge quickly all you have on — .	Pertendo
— has cracked *heel*	Pertexo
— has been sent *home* . . .	Pertinax
— will be *knocked* out . . .	Pervinco
Do you *know* anything for — .	Pervius
— dead-*lame* after exercise . .	Pestifer
— is *lame*	Petalium
— is reported *lame*	Petaso
Lay the odds to £5 against — .	Petiolus
Lay the odds to £10 against — .	Pexatus
Lay the odds to £15 against — .	Phani
Lay the odds to £20 against — .	Phaselus
Lay the odds to £25 against — .	Phasma
Lay the odds to £30 against — .	Phellos
Lay the odds to £35 against — .	Phiditia
Lay the odds to £40 against — .	Phormion
Lay the odds to £45 against — .	Phragmis
Lay the odds to £50 against — .	Phycos
Lay the odds to £55 against — .	Phylaca
Lay the odds to £60 against — .	Phyllon
Lay the odds to £70 against — .	Physema
Lay the odds to £80 against — .	Piaculum
Lay the odds to £90 against — .	Pignero
Lay the odds to £100 against — .	Pigritia
Lay the odds to £150 against — .	Pinaster
Lay the odds to £200 against — .	Pineta
Lay the odds to £250 against — .	Pistacia
Lay the odds to £300 against — .	Pityusa
Lay the odds to £400 against — .	Placenta
Lay the odds to £500 against — .	Placidus
Lay the odds to £600 against — .	Plagiger
Lay the odds to £7.00 against — .	Plagosus

Lay the odds to £800 against —	Planipes
Lay the odds to £900 against —	Plantago
Lay the odds to £1,000 against —	Pleiades
Lay the odds to £2,000 against —	Plinthus
Lay the odds to £3,000 against —	Plorator
Lay the odds to £4,000 against —	Plumatus
Lay the odds to £5,000 against —	Plumbo
Lay over your book against —	Plumesco
Lay your book only against —	Pluvius
Cannot *lay* at any price	Podager
Cease *laying* against —	Podex
Good men are *laying* —	Podium
Market arranged, do not *lay*	Poetica
Succeeded in *laying* for you —	Pogonias
— has hit its *leg*	Politicus
— reported to have *leg* filled	Polygala
— is only a *market* horse	Pomosus
— has the *mount,* and fancies it	Pompa
— has the *mount,* but does not fancy it	Pondero
Money is right with —	Ponto
Money is wrong with —	Popina
Answer what *odds* you have obtained	Poples
— has not been *out* to-day	Populus
— is a good *outsider*	Portatus
— is the best *outsider*	Positio
Owner cannot get on, public got the money	Possedi
Owner does not fancy	Possunt
Owner fancies —	Postmodo
— is sure to get a *place*	Postpono
Put me £1 to win on —	Postquam
Put me £1 to win, and £1 for a place on —	Potior
Put me £2 to win on —	Potorius
Put me £2 to win, and £2 for a place on —	Pransito
Put me £3 to win on —	Pratulum
Put me £3 to win, and £3 for a place on —	Pravitas
Put me £4 to win on —	Precario

Put me £4 to win, and £4 for a place on — .	Prehendo
Put me £5 to win on —	Pretiose
Put me £5 to win, and £5 for a place on —	Pridianus
Put me £6 to win on —.	Primum
Put me £6 to win, and £6 for a place on —	Princeps
Put me £7 to win on —	Privatim
Put me £7 to win, and £7 for a place on —	Proavia
Put me £8 to win on —	Probatio
Put me £8 to win, and £8 for a place on —	Problema
Put me £9 to win on —	Probum
Put me £9 to win, and £9 for a place on —	Procax
Put me £10 to win on —	Proclamo
Put me £10 to win, and £10 for a place on—	Proculco
Put me £20 to win on —	Procumbo
Put me £25 to win on —	Procuro
Put me £30 to win on —	Prodige
Put me £35 to win on —	Prodere
Put me £40 to win on —	Proditur
Put me £45 to win on —	Profano
Put me £50 to win on —	Profaris
Put me £60 to win on —	Profindo
Put me £70 to win on —	Prohibeo
Put me £75 to win on —	Prolabor
Put me £100 to win on —.	Proles
Put me £200 to win on —. . . .	Prolixe
Put me £300 to win on —. . . .	Prolixus
Put me £400 to win on —. . . .	Proludo
Put me £500 to win on —. . . .	Prompto
Put me £1,000 to win on — . . .	Promulgo
What do you *recommend* . . .	Pronecto
Am waiting here for your *reply* . .	Pronepos
— has been *retained* to ride — . .	Pronomen
— is all *right*, no cause for apprehension .	Pronubus
— *runs*, and is meant to win. . .	Propalam
— is sure not to *run*	Propello
— is sure to *run*	Propense

— will *run,* but do not fancy it . . .	Propior
The number of *runners* will be at least — .	Propola
The number of *runners* will probably be about —	Proposui
— should be kept on the *safe side* . .	Proprie
— is *scratched*	Proptosis
— is not *scratched* as reported . .	Propulso
— is reported *scratched*	Proreta
Succeeded in *taking* for you — . . .	Prorogo
Trial was genuine	Proserpo
Trial was not genuine	Prosilio
— has been *tried,* and beaten . . .	Prospere
— has been *tried,* and beaten by — .	Prospexi
— has been *tried,* and won easily, beating —	Prosterno
— has been *tried,* and won, stable is satisfied	Prosto
— took *walking* exercise only . . .	Prosum
Think something is *wrong* with — . .	Protelum

Races, List of Important.

N.B.—All Races having names limited to one word, such as Derby, Oaks, Cesarewitch, &c., are purposely omitted in this list.

Alexandra Plate, *Ascot*	Protendo
Ascot Gold Cup	Proterve
Champagne Stakes, *Doncaster* . .	Protollo
Chesterfield Cup, *Goodwood* . .	Protraho
Chesterfield Stakes, *Newmarket* . .	Protrudo
City and Suburban Handicap . .	Protypum
Earl Spencer's Plate, *Northampton* .	Provenio
French Derby	Providus
French Oaks	Provoco
Gold Cup, *Epsom*	Proxime
Goodwood Cup	Pruina
Goodwood Stakes	Prunum
Grand Prix de Paris	Pruritus

Great Challenge Stakes (*Newmarket* Second October)	Prytanis
Jockey Club Cup (*Newmarket Houghton*) .	Psaltria
Liverpool Grand National	Psegma
Middle Park Plate	Psora
New Stakes, *Ascot*	Psyllion
Newmarket October Handicap . . .	Pucinum
One Thousand Guineas . . .	Pudicum
Prince of Wales's Stakes, *Ascot* . . .	Puellas
Rous Memorial Stakes, *Ascot* . . .	Pueritia
Royal Hunt Cup, *Ascot* . . .	Pugillar
St. Leger Stakes, *Doncaster* . . .	Pugillum
Two Thousand Guineas . . .	Pugnator

Railway. (Refer to ACCIDENT, ENQUIRE, PARCEL, SEND, TRAIN.)

Ready at a moment's notice	Pulcher
Am quite *ready* to start . . .	Pulecium
Please hold yourself *ready* to start .	Pulex
When will you be *ready* . . .	Pullulo

Reduction is asked to the extent of — .	Pulmo
Endeavour to get a *reduction* . .	Pulsatio
What *reduction* can be made . .	Pulvinar
What *reduction* is asked for . .	Pumilus

(Refer)—You may *refer* to	Punctus

References are satisfactory . . .	Punitio
References are not satisfactory . .	Purifico
Our *references* are —. . . .	Pustula
Further *references* are necessary . .	Putamen
What *references* can you give . .	Putealis

Remain at home	Putredo

Remain at home for me	Putresco
Remain at home, will call this evening .	Putror
Remain there for the present . .	Pyralis
Remain there until I come . . .	Pyrgus
Remain there until — . . .	Pyrites
Am I to *remain* here	Pyropus
Better *remain* —	Pythia
Better *remain* a few days . . .	Pythicus
Better *remain* another day . . .	Rabidus
Better *remain*, as you suggest . .	Rabiose
Better *remain* there for the present .	Radicor
How long am I to *remain* . . .	Radicula
How long will you *remain* . . .	Radiosus
Likely to *remain* here a few days .	Radius
Likely to *remain* here another week .	Ramale
Likely to *remain* here another fortnight	Ramex
Likely to *remain* here another month .	Ramosior
Likely to *remain* here to-day . .	Ranceo
Likely to *remain* here until — . .	Raptio
Must *remain* here until — . . .	Raritas

Remittance. (Refer to Acknowledge, Cheque, Money, Place.)

Remittance has been sent as requested .	Raritatis
Remittance is not yet to hand . .	Raritudo
Remittance is to hand. . . .	Rasito
Cannot *remit* before — . . .	Rastrum
Cannot *remit* more than — . . .	Raucitas
Have *remitted* as requested £ — .	Ravem
Have *remitted* to the credit of — .	Ravis
What amount have you *remitted* . .	Reapse
When will you *remit*	Reatus

Renew. (See Acceptance.)

Repairs are in progress, but not yet completed . Rebellis

Repairs will be completed by — .	Recalco
Can it be *repaired*	Recalvus
Can you *repair*	Recenter
Damage is *repaired*	Receptio
Do not do any *repairs* . . .	Receptus
Shall I have it *repaired* . . .	Rechamus
What *repairs* are required . . .	Recingo
What will the *repairs* cost . . .	Recinium
When will *repairs* be completed . .	Recito

Reply.   (Refer to LETTERS, ORDER, TELEGRAM.)

Reply as soon as possible . . .	Reclivis
Reply by letter	Recludit
Reply by messenger . . .	Recludo
Reply by telegram . . .	Recludunt
Reply cannot be given for a few days .	Reclusi
Reply shall be sent by post to-day .	Reclusus
Reply shall be sent by telegram . .	Recogito
Reply shall be sent in a few days .	Recoquo
Reply shall be sent next mail . .	Recordor
Reply shall be sent to-morrow .	Recreatum
Cannot understand why you do not *reply* .	Recreavi
Reply has not yet come to hand . .	Recupero

Report is not correct	Recurso
Report is quite correct . . .	Recurvus
Send further *report* immediately. .	Redactus

(Represent)—Will *represent* me in the matter .	Redamo

Request cannot be complied with . .	Redarguo
Request will be complied with . .	Redditio

Resolution was carried by a large majority .	Redhibeo
Resolution was carried by a small majority .	Redimio

Resolution was carried unanimously .	**Reditum**
Resolution was lost by a large majority .	**Redoleo**
Resolution was lost by a small majority .	**Redormio**
It has been *resolved* that — . . .	**Redundo**

(Responsibility)—Accept the *responsibility* .	**Reduvia**
Cannot accept the *responsibility* . . .	**Redux**
Refuses to be *responsible*	**Refectio**
Who is *responsible*	**Refector**
Who will be *responsible*	**Refercio**
You are *responsible*	**Reflatus**
You are not *responsible*	**Reflecto**

Result is in favour of —	**Refodio**
Result is not yet known	**Reformo**
Result is satisfactory	**Refragor**
Result is unsatisfactory	**Refregi**
Result will not be known for a few days .	**Refringo**
Result will probably be in favour of — .	**Refugium**
Let me know the *result* of — . .	**Refugus**
Let me know the *result* of the election .	**Regalis**
Let me know the *result* of the match . .	**Regelo**
Let me know the *result* of the meeting .	**Regie**
Let me know the *result* of the race .	**Regifice**
Let me know the *result* of your enquiries .	**Regimen**
Let me know the *result* of your interview .	**Regno**

Return at once	**Regnum**
Return at once, all arranged satisfactorily .	**Regulus**
Return at once, all shall be arranged as you desire	**Regusto**
Return at once, or consequences will be serious	**Regyro**
Better *return* —	**Rehalo**
Better *return* to-day	**Reice**
Better *return* to-morrow	**Rejectus**

Shall *return* in time for dinner .   .   .   **Relabor**
Shall *return* in time for dinner, am bringing — **Relatio**

Sample has arrived.   .   .   .   .   **Relaxus**
  Sample has been sent.   .   .   .   **Relictum**
  Sample has not arrived   .   .   .   **Relino**
  Sample will be sent .   .   .   .   **Reliquus**
  Forward another *sample*   .   .   .   **Reluctor**
  Forward by post *sample* and price of — .   **Remano**
  When will *sample* be sent .   .   .   **Remansio**

Security offered is accepted   .   .   .   **Remex**
  Security offered is not accepted .   .   **Remigium**
  Better *security* is required .   .   .   **Remisceo**
  Can you obtain good *security*   .   .   **Remissus**
  Get the best *security* you can   .   .   **Remolior**
  What *security* have you obtained   .   .   **Remoram**

(Sell)—At what price may I *sell* .   .   .   **Remordeo**
  Do not *sell* at any price   .   .   .   **Remotus**
  Do not *sell* at less than —   .   .   **Remugio**
  Do not *sell* until further orders .   .   **Remunero**

Send as early as possible .   .   .   .   **Renarro**
  Send at once by — .   .   .   .   **Renatus**
  Send at once by cheque   .   .   .   **Renavigo**
  Send at once by quickest means — .   **Renendus**
  Send at once by P.O.O. —   .   .   **Renixus**
  Send at once by Parcel Post   .   .   **Reno**
  Send at once by post .   .   .   .   **Renuntio**
  Send at once by railway goods train .   **Renuntius**
  Send at once by railway passenger train .   **Repandus**
  Send at once by Great Eastern Railway Co. **Reparco**
  Send at once by Great Northern Railway Co. **Repecto**
  Send at once by Great Western Railway Co. **Repente**

Send at once by London, Brighton, and South Coast Railway Co. . . .	**Repertor**
Send at once by London, Chatham, and Dover Railway Co.	**Repexus**
Send at once by London and North-Western Railway Co.	**Repletus**
Send at once by London and South-Western Railway Co.	**Replico**
Send at once by Midland Railway Co. .	**Replum**
Send at once by South Eastern Railway Co.	**Replumbo**
Send at once by special messenger . .	**Repono**
Send at once with the goods already on order	**Reportare**
Send authority to —	**Reporto**
Send authority for —	**Repostus**
Send authority at once	**Repotia**
Send for enclosure to-day to — . . .	**Repotiorum**
Send for enclosure to-morrow to — . .	**Repressi**
Send full instructions. . . .	**Repressor**
Send full particulars of — . . .	**Reprobo**
Send full particulars of accident . . .	**Reptatio**
Send full particulars of claim . . .	**Repudio**
Send full particulars of damage . . .	**Repudium**
Send my evening dress here . . .	**Repugno**
Send my evening dress to — . . .	**·Repulsus**
Send my flannels here	**Repurgo**
Send my flannels to —	**Reputo** .
Send to our order at Railway Station at —.	**Reputabo**
Send to our order at Railway Station here .	**Reputans**
Send to our order at wharf here . . .	**Reputavi**
Have *sent* as requested	**Requies**
Have *sent* by special messenger . . .	**Requiro**
Have *sent* by Great Eastern Railway Co. .	**Resaluto**
Have *sent* by Great Northern Railway Co. .	**Resarcio**
Have *sent* by Great Western Railway Co. .	**Resecro**

Have *sent* by London, Brighton, and South
    Coast Railway Co. . . . . . Resectus
Have *sent* by London, Chatham, and Dover
    Railway Co. . . . . . Resedo
Have *sent* by London and North-Western
    Railway Co. . . . . . Resegmen
Have *sent* by London and South-Western
    Railway Co. . . . . . Resemino
Have *sent* by Midland Railway Co. . . Resequor
Have *sent* by South-Eastern Railway Co. . Reservo

(**Service**) — Will you take *service* for me
    on — . . . . Residuus
Will you take *service* for me on Sunday . Resignat
Will you take *service* for me to-morrow . Resilio

(**Settle**)—Cannot *settle* at present, will do so
    shortly . . . . . . Resistit
Everything *settled*, return at once . . Resolvo
Everything *settled*, telegraph when you will
    come . . . . . . Resonus
Settlement arrived at satisfactorily . . Resorbeo
Settlement is impossible . . . . Resorpsi
Settlement must be come to . . . Respergo
Settlement must be come to immediately . Respiro
Settlement must be come to by — . . Restagno

Ship is detained in quarantine . . . Restillo
Ship is detained in port . . . . Restiti
Ship is due on the — . . . . Restringo
Ship is just leaving port . . . . Resudo
Ship sailed from here on the — . . . Resulto
Ship will sail on the — . . . . Resupiño
What is the name of the *ship* . . . Resurgo
When did the *ship* arrive . . . . Retardo
When was the *ship* last heard of . . . Retectus

(Size)—What is about the *size* . . .	.	Retego
What *size* do you want	.	Retentio

Sold by order of the Court . . .	.	Retexui
Sold by public auction	.	Reticeo
Sold with all faults	.	Retono
For how much has it been *sold* . .	.	Retostus
It has been *sold* for — . . .	.	Retribuo
Was not *sold*	.	Retroago
Will not be *sold*	.	Retrudo

(Standstill)—Am quite at a *standstill* .	.	Retrusus

(Start)—Cannot *start* at time agreed on .	.	Reunctor
Cannot *start* to-day	.	Reus
Cannot *start* until —. . . .	.	Reveho

Statement is confirmed	.	Revera
Statement is denied	.	Reversus
Statement is incorrect, send another . .	.	Revincio
Full *statement* sent by post . .	.	Revisito
Send *statement* of account . . .	.	Revocatio
You are authorised to deny the *statement*	.	Revocare

Stock is abundant	.	Revulsi
Stock is very low	.	Rhacinus
What have you in *stock* . . .	.	Rhacoma

Subject to a discount of — . . .	.	Rhagion
Subject to analysis	.	Rhamnus
Subject to your approval . . .	.	Rhetor

Sufficient time must be given . . .	.	Rhexia
Is not *sufficient*	.	Rhodora
Is quite *sufficient*	.	Rhoicus

G

(Suit)—It will not *suit* . . . . . Rhombus
It will *suit* very well . . . . . Rhyas

Supply is exhausted . . . . . Rhytion
Send a further *supply* of — . . . Rigatio

Sympathise deeply with you in the loss you
 have sustained . . . . . Rigesco
 Sympathise deeply with you in your trouble . Rigide

(Take)—Do not *take* — . . . . . Rigidor
How long will it *take* . . . . Rigoris
How long will it *take* to complete . . Riparius
Refuse to *take* it back . . . . Ritualis
When will it *take* place . . . . Rixator
Will *take* it into consideration . . . Rixosus
Will *take* it with me . . . . . Roboreus

Telegram. (Refer to Acknowledge, Address,
 Cancel, Hotels, Order, Unicode,
 Wait.)
Telegram received . . . . . Roboro
Telegram received, agree to — . . . Robur
Telegram received, agree to your terms . Robustus
Telegram received, cannot agree to contents . Rodo
Telegram received, cannot agree to terms,
 will write . . . . Rogalem
Telegram received, cannot agree to your
 terms . . . . Rogator
Telegram received, cannot cancel orders . Rogito
Telegram received, cannot cancel orders,
 already attended to . . . . Roresco
Telegram received, cannot do so . . . Rorifer
Telegram received, cannot do so to-day. ∴ Rosetum
Telegram received, cannot meet you . . Rosmaris

Telegram received, cannot meet you until —	**Rotatus**
Telegram received, cannot understand its meaning, wire again in different words .	**Rotula**
Telegram received, have done as you requested	**Rotundus**
Telegram received, have written you fully .	**Rubellus**
Telegram received, meeting postponed . .	**Rubesco**
Telegram received, meeting postponed until —	**Rubetum**
Telegram received, orders cancelled . .	**Rubia**
Telegram received, orders cancelled, and subsequent ones substituted . . .	**Rubrica**
Telegram received too late	**Rudis**
Telegram received too late for — . .	**Rufulus**
Telegram received too late for post . .	**Rugosus**
Telegram received, will meet you . .	**Ruidus**
Telegram received, will meet you at — .	**Ruiturus**
Telegram received, will meet you as desired .	**Rumpus**
Telegram received, will do as you wish .	**Runcator**
Telegram and letter received . . .	**Runcina**
Telegram and letter received, having attention	**Runco**
Telegram and letter received, having attention, will write	**Ruptor**
Our last *telegram* was dated — . . .	**Ruralis**
Reply immediately to *telegram* sent on — .	**Rursum**
There is no *telegram* from you here, wire to me at once to —	**Rurum**
There is no *telegram* from you here, wire to me at once to this address . .	**Ruscario**
There is no *telegram* from you here, wire to me to Poste Restante at — . .	**Ruscarium**
There is no *telegram* from you here, wire to me to Poste Restante here . .	**Ruscum**
Telegraph date despatched	**Russatus**
Telegraph date of departure . . .	**Rustice**
Telegraph him [or her] at Poste Restante — .	**Rusticitas**
Telegraph how many are wanted . .	**Rusticor**
Telegraph me at Poste Restante — . .	**Ruta**

G 2

Telegraph me at Poste Restante here . .	**Rutarum**
Telegraph present price of — . . .	**Sabulo**
Telegraph reply to letter	**Sacal**
Telegraph reply to letter of — . . .	**Sacco**
Telegraph result of —	**Sacculus**
Telegraph result of your interview . .	**Sacellum**
Telegraph substance of your letter . .	**Sacodios**
Telegraph what progress you are making .	**Sacoma**
Telegraph your address for letters to be posted to you to-night	**Sacomatis**
Telegraph your address for letters to be posted to you to-morrow . . .	**Sacrarium**
Telegraph your address for letters to be posted to you on —	**Sacratum**

Terms. (Refer to Telegram.)

Terms are accepted	**Sacrifer**
Terms are considered satisfactory . . .	**Sacris**
Terms are rejected	**Sagatus**
Terms are too high	**Sagdarum**
Terms are too low	**Saginatio**
Terms will not suit	**Sagminis**
Accept the *terms* offered	**Sagulum**
Cannot accept other *terms* than already named	**Sagum**
Get the best *terms* possible	**Salacia**
Get the best *terms* possible, and wire result .	**Salarius**
What are the best *terms*	**Salebra**
What are your *terms*	**Salgama**
What *terms* are agreed to	**Salictum**

(Thanks)—Accept our best *thanks* . . . **Salignus**

Theatre, or Concert.

Book a private box for the — . . .	**Salillum**
Book a private box for this evening . .	**Salina**
Book one stall for —	**Saliunca**

Book two stalls for —	Salivosus
Book three stalls for —	Salsius
Book four stalls for —	Salsura
Book one dress circle seat for —	Saltatio
Book two dress circle seats for —	Saltem
Book three dress circle seats for —	Saluber
Book four dress circle seats for —	Saluto
Book one upper circle seat for —	Sambuca
Book two upper circle seats for —	Samiolus
Book three upper circle seats for —	Samnites
Book four upper circle seats for —	Sandalis
Cannot get tickets	Sandyx
Cannot get tickets you want	Sanesco
Cannot get tickets you want, shall I take for —	Sangenon
Have a private box for to-night for the —	Sanguino
Have stalls for to-night for the —	Sanitas
Have dress circle tickets for to-night for the	Santerna
Have upper circle tickets for to-night for the	Saperda
Have tickets for to-night for the —	Sapineus
Received *invitation* for concert this evening at—	Sapros
Received *invitation* for concert this evening, can you come	Sarcina
Received *invitation* for theatre this evening	Sardonyx
Received *invitation* for theatre this evening, can you come	Sarissa
Received *invitation* for theatre this evening, meet me at —	Sarmen
Shall I take a box for the —	Sarritio
Shall I take stalls for the —	Sartago
Shall I take tickets for the —	Satageus
Take a box for to-night for the —	Satagito
Take stalls for to-night for the —	Satisdo
Take dress circle seats for to-night for the —	Sativus
Take upper circle seats for to-night for the —	Satura
Take tickets for to-night for the —	Saucius

There ought to be . . . . . . Saxifer
    There ought not to be . . . . Scaber
    There will be . . . . . . Scabres
    There will not be . . . . . Scala

Time has already expired . . . . Scalprum
    Time is too long . . . . . Scambus
    Time is too short . . . . . Scamnum
    Time must be made the essence of the con-
       tract . . . . Scando
    Time will expire on the — . . . Scansilis
    Can you alter the *time* to— . . . Scarifico
    Can you extend the *time* for —. . . Scarites
    Shall I be in *time* for — . . . Scatebra
    There is not sufficient *time* . . . Scena
    There will be plenty of *time* . . Scheda
    What is the latest *time* for — . . Schidius

Too long to telegraph details, am writing fully . Schiston

(Train)—Have missed *train* . . . . Scholium
    Have missed *train*, cannot arrive in time
      for — . . . . Scienter
    Have missed *train*, cannot arrive this evening Scilicet
    Have missed *train*, cannot arrive until — . Scincus
    Have missed *train*, do not expect me . . Scio
    Have missed *train*, impossible to be home
      before — . . . . . . Scirpeus
    Have missed *train*, impossible to be with
      you to-night . . . . Scirroma
    Have missed *train*, make other arrangements Scloppus
    Have missed *train*, postpone meeting . . Scobina
    Have missed *train*, postpone meeting until— Scolymos
    Have missed *train*, remaining here to-night Scombrus
    Have missed *train*, send carriage to meet me
      at — . . . . Screatus

Have missed *train,* send conveyance to meet me at —	Scrinium
Have missed *train,* shall arrive later . .	Scriptio
Have missed *train,* unable to keep appointment	Scrofula
Have missed *train,* wait for me until — .	Scutatus
Have missed *train,* wait until I arrive .	Scutella
Have missed *train,* will come by first in the morning	Scutica
Leaving by *train* arriving at — . . .	Scyphus
Leaving by *train* arriving at Cannon Street Station at —	Scyricum
Leaving by *train* arriving at Charing Cross Station at —	Scytala
Leaving by *train* arriving at Euston at — .	Scythica
Leaving by *train* arriving at Fenchurch Street at —	Secedo
Leaving by *train* arriving at Holborn Viaduct at —	Secessio
Leaving by *train* arriving at King's Cross at —	Secius
Leaving by *train* arriving at Liverpool Street at —	Secludo
Leaving by *train* arriving at London Bridge at —	Secretio
Leaving by *train* arriving at Paddington at —	Secundum
Leaving by *train* arriving at St. Pancras at —	Sedecula
Leaving by *train* arriving at Victoria at — .	Seduco
Leaving by *train* arriving at Waterloo at —	Segestre
Leaving by *train* due at — . . .	Segnipes
Leaving by *train,* meet me at —. . .	Segnis
Leaving by *train,* meet me at station at — .	Segnitia
Leaving by *train,* send carriage to meet me at —	Segrego

Leaving by *train*, send conveyance to meet
me at — . . . . . . Segullum
Leaving by *train*, shall be with you at — . Sejungo
Leaving by *train* this afternoon . . . Selago
Leaving by *train* this evening . . . Selectio
Leaving by *train* this morning . . . Selibra

(**Trial**)—When will the *trial* take place . . Sella

(**Trouble**)—Do not *trouble* in the matter . . Sellaria
Will necessitate too much *trouble* . . Sementis

(**True**)—It is not *true* . . . . . Semibos
It is quite *true* . . . . . . Semidea

(**Trusted**)—Are they to be *trusted* . . . Semihora
Can be *trusted* to the extent of — . . Seminex
Do not *trust* — . . . . . Semito
To what extent can they be *trusted* . . Semodius

(**Understand**)—Do not *understand* your letter . Semoveo
Do not *understand* your telegram . . Semuncia
Do you *understand* . . . . . Semustus
Do you *understand* our meaning. . . Senecio
Does he *understand* . . . . . Senectus

(**Unicode**)—To decipher this message refer to
the UNICODE . . . . . Unicode

(**Unnecessary**)—Consider it *unnecessary* . . Senex

(**Unsaleable**)—Is *unsaleable*, unless at a heavy loss Senium
Is quite *unsaleable* . . . . . Sentisco

Unsatisfactory reports have arrived . . Seorsum
Is very *unsatisfactory* . . . . Sepelio

Visit. (Refer to APPOINTMENTS, POSTPONE, TRAIN.)

Wait for me at —	Septicus
Wait for me this evening	Sereno
Wait for me this evening, will call . .	Sergia
Wait my arrival	Seriola
Wait my letter before starting . .	Serius
Wait my letter before taking any action .	Serratim
Wait my telegram before starting .	Sesqui
Wait my telegram before taking any action	Sessito
Wait until you hear further before —. .	Sestiana
Wait until you receive my letter . .	Setanium
Am *waiting* here for a letter from you before starting	Setosus
Am *waiting* here for a telegram from you before starting	Sevoco
Weather too unfavourable	Sexatruus
Weather too unfavourable, do not come .	Sextiana
Weather too unfavourable, must postpone —	Sextula
Weather too unfavourable, return by rail .	Sexus
Weather too unfavourable, returning by next train	Siccanus
Weather too unfavourable to put to sea .	Siccine
Weather too unfavourable to put to sea, will telegraph departure . . .	Siderior
Weather too unfavourable to start to-day .	Sido
Weather very fine	Sigma
Weather very fine, excursion to-day .	Signifer
Weather very fine, sea quite smooth .	Signinus
Weather very fine, shall expect you—. .	Signum
Weather very fine, shall expect you this morning	Silaceus
Weather very fine, shall expect you this afternoon	Siliqua

Weather very fine, shall expect you this evening	Silurus
Weather very fine, shall start to-day . .	Silva
Weather very fine, will wait your arrival .	Silvesco

When did you last hear from — . . . Silvicola

Will. (Refer to DEATHS, EXECUTORS.)

Writing. (Refer to LETTER, POST.)

Writing to you by to-day's post . . .	Similago
Writing to you by early post . . .	Similis
Writing to you by next mail — . . .	Simplex
Writing you to-day respecting — . .	Simultas
Writing you to-morrow respecting — .	Sinciput

(Wrong)—Is anything *wrong* . . . . Sindon

Is anything *wrong*, have received nothing from —	Singulus
Is anything *wrong*, have not heard from you	Sinister
Is anything *wrong*, have not heard from you for some time	Sinopis
Nothing *wrong*, will write	Sinum

Wrote. (Refer to LETTER, POST.)

Wrote to you addressed to — . . .	Sinuosus
Wrote to you by mail of last — . .	Siparium
Wrote to you by this evening's post .	Siquandare
Wrote to you by this morning's post .	Siquando

PRIVATE CODE.

A SIMPLE means of converting the Unicode into a secret private code is for correspondents to arrange to use instead of the cypher set opposite to the phrases in the book the cypher affixed to the phrase one, two, or more lines above or below, as may be selected. For instance, if it is agreed to use instead of the regulation cypher word the one next following it in the Code, a telegram with the word "*Oporice*" would mean to the general body of Unicode users "Posted letter to-day, do not leave before receipt;" but the person for whose private information the message was intended would read the real meaning as "Posted letter to-day, do not act on it, another follows."

The following selection of cypher words will never be included in the "Unicode" for permanent use with any specific phrases. They are intended to be used only for private phrases to be arranged specially between individual correspondents :—

Veneno

Venenum

Venereus

Veneror

Venetus

Venicula

Venor

Venosus

Ventilo

Ventrale

Venundo

Venus

Vepres

Vepretum

Veratrum

Verax

Verbena

Verber

Verbosus

Veredus

Veretrum

Veritas

Vermino

Vermis

Vernatio

Verpus

Verrinus

Verruca

Versoria

Vertagus

Vertebra

Vertigo

Verum

Verutum

Vesania

Vescor

Vesica

Vesicula

Vesper

Vestio

Vestras

Veto

Vetulus

Vetustas

Vexatio

Vexator

Vexillum

Vialis

Viarius

Viaticus

Viator

Vibex

Vibro

Vicarius

Vicatim

Vicinia

Vicissim

Victima

Victito

Victrix

Vidi

Viduitas

Vidulum

Viduus

Vigesco

Vigil

Vigilax

Vigilia

Vigor

Villa

Villaris

Villicus

Villula

Vimen

Vinaceus

Vinca

Vincio

Vinctura

Vincales

Vindemia

Vindex

Vindico

Vinetum

Vinitor

Viola

Violator

Violens

Violenter

Vipera

Vipereus

Virago

Viresco

Viretum

Virgula

Viridis

Viritim

Virosus

Virtus

Visula

Vix

The following cypher words have been added to "Unicode" since its first publication :—

Antidotum	Obvigilo
Anxiferum	Obviam
Congruum	Obvolvunt
Conifer	Occallatus
Coniferum	Occano
Mellilla	Occasiones
Mellinia	Orarum
Mellis	Palpaminum
Mellitorum	Palpare
Mellitum	Palpat
Mello	Palpamus
Mellorum	Palpandum
Mellum	Raritatis
Melofolia	Ravem
Melofoliam	Recludit
Meminisse	Recludo
Memoris	Recludunt
Memoratus	Reportare
Obvertunto	Repotiorum
Obvigilat	Repressi
Obvigilavi	Reputabo

H

Reputans

Reputavi

Rotula

Rurum

Ruscario

Ruscarium

Ruscum

Rusticitas

Ruta

Rutarum

Sacomatis

Sacrarium

Sacratum

Sinuosus

Siparium

Siquandare

Siquando

UNICODE USERS.

The following is a List of important firms and establishments to whom messages in the "Unicode" may be sent by any persons at any time without necessity for previous arrangement. Their registered telegraphic address is also given.

NAME OF FIRM.	REGISTERED TELEGRAPHIC ADDRESS.
Addams-Williams, R., 16, Commercial Street, Newport, Monmouth (and at Crickhowell)	Addams-Williams, Newport, Mon.
Alabaster, Passmore & Sons, Fann Street, Aldersgate Street, London	Alamores, London.
Allan Brothers & Co., Allan Royal Mail Line, 103, Leaden-hall Street, London	Allanline, London.
"Anchor" Line (see Henderson Brothers).	
Anglo-American Brush Electric Light Corporation, Limited, Belvedere Road, London	Magneto, London.
Anglo-American Rope and Oakum Company, 12, Hopwood Street, Liverpool	Oakum, Liverpool.
Army and Navy Co-operative Society, Limited, 117, Victoria Street, London	Army, London.
Arnold, E. J., 3, Briggate, Leeds	Arnold, Leeds.
Artistic Stationery Co., Limited, Plough Court, Fetter Lane, London	Artistic, London.
Bain, W., & Co., 6a, Victoria Street, Westminster, London.	Lochrin, London.
Edinburgh	Lochrin, Edinburgh.
Baird, William & Co., 168, West George Street, Glasgow.	Bairds, Glasgow.
Ballantyne, Hanson & Co., 4, Chandos Street, Charing Cross, London	Ballantyne Press, London.
Edinburgh : Paul's Work	Ballantyne Press, Edinburgh.
Bemrose & Sons, 23, Old Bailey, London	Bemrose, London.
Derby	Bemrose, Derby.
Binnie, James, 69, Bath Street, Glasgow.	Gartcosh, Glasgow.
Binns, Walter, Stanhope Works, Horton Lane, Bradford	Stanhope, Bradford.
Bird, Bookseller, Tring.	Bird, Tring.
Bollans, E., & Co., Ranelagh Works, Leamington.	Bollans, Leamington.
Brandauer, C., & Co., Steel Pen Works, New John Street West, Birmingham.	Brandauer, Birmingham.
Brendon, William, & Son, Printers, Plymouth.	Brendonson, Plymouth.
Brinsmead, John, & Sons, 18, 20, and 22, Wigmore Street, London	Brinsmead, London.
Brown's Hotel (J. J. Ford & Sons), 22, Dover Street, London	Brownotel, London.
Brown, Scott & Co., Red Lion Yard, 254, High Holborn, London	Punctual, London.
Brown, A., & Sons, 26 and 27, Savile Street, Hull.	Brown, Hull.
Bull, William James, 21, Westcroft Square, Ravenscourt Park, Hammersmith, London ; National Union Club, Albemarle Street ; and London Sailing Club.	

NAME OF FIRM.	REGISTERED TELEGRAPHIC ADDRESS.
Bullivant & Co., 72, Mark Lane, London	Bullivants, London.
Caldwell Brothers, Limited, Waterloo Stationery and Printing Works, 11, 13, and 15, Waterloo Place, Edinburgh	Caldwells, Edinburgh.
Callender's Bitumen, Telegraph and Waterproof Co., Limited, 101, Leadenhall Street, London	Callender, London.
Cameron & Ferguson, 88, West Nile Street, Glasgow	Exemplum, Glasgow.
London : Salisbury Court, Fleet Street	Cameronius, London.
Cammell, Charles, & Co., Limited, Cyclops Steel and Iron Works, Sheffield	Cammell, Sheffield.
Campbell, P. and P., The Perth Dye Works, Perth	Campbell, Perth.
Carter, F. & F. W., Chartered Accountants, 5, St. Andrew's Square, Edinburgh	Carter, Edinburgh.
Cassell & Co., Limited, La Belle Sauvage, Ludgate Hill, London	Caspeg, London.
Causton, Sir Joseph, & Sons, 9, Eastcheap, London	Caustcheap, London.
Chatwood's Patent Safe and Lock Co., Limited, 76, Newgate Street, London	Chatwoods, London.
Manchester : 11, Cross Street	Chatwoods, Manchester.
Liverpool : 17, Lord Street	Chatwoods, Liverpool.
Leeds : 22, Bond Street	Chatwoods, Leeds.
Bolton : Lancashire Safe and Lock Works	Chatwoods, Bolton.
Chubb & Son's Lock and Safe Company, Limited, 128, Queen Victoria Street, London.	Chubb, London.
City Timber & Saw Mills Co., Limited, 168, London Road, Liverpool. (P. Macmuldrow, Managing Director.)	Macmuldrow, Liverpool.
Civil Service Supply Association, Limited, 136, Queen Victoria Street, London	Stores, London.
Clabburn, James, Norwich	
Clay & Abraham, 87, Bold Street, Liverpool	One, Liverpool.
Clay Cross Company, The, Clay Cross Collieries, near Chesterfield	Jackson, Clay Cross.
Clode, A. O., Letchmore Heath, Elstree	Clode, Radlett.
Coates & Co., Blackfriars Distillery, Plymouth.	Coates, Plymouth.
Cochrane, Paterson & Co., Leith	Cochrane, Leith.
Cochrane, Thos. E., Lieutenant, H. M. S. *Invincible*, Southampton.	
Collingridge, W. H. and L., City Press, 148 and 149, Aldersgate Street, London	Collingridge, London.
Collings, J.A., Monce Square, and Richmond Walk, Devonport	Jacoals, Devonport.
Colville, David, & Sons, 7, Fenchurch Avenue, London	Colville, Motherwell.
Conacher, James, & Sons, Bath Buildings, Organ Works, Huddersfield	Ericht, Huddersfield.
Conan, Joseph, 4, Dawson Street, Dublin.	Conan, Dublin.
Cook, Son & Co., 22, St. Paul's Churchyard, London	Cook, St. Paul's, London.
Coope, E. Jesser, S.S. Yacht *Sunrise*.	
Corrie, William, & Co., 114, 116, 118, and 120, Cromac Street, Belfast	Cromac, Belfast.
Cotterell Brothers, 11, Clare Street, Bristol	Cotterells, Bristol.
Couper, James, & Sons, City Glass Works, Glasgow	Coupers, Glasgow.
Coventry Cycle Company, White Friars Lane, Coventry	Imperial, Coventry.
Coventry Machinists' Company, Limited, 15 and 16, Holborn Viaduct, London	Cheylsmore, London.
Cowie Brothers & Co., 59, St. Vincent Street, Glasgow	Celtic, Glasgow.

NAME OF FIRM.	REGISTERED TELEGRAPHIC ADDRESS.
Crossley, John, & Sons, Limited:—	
Halifax : Dean Clough Mills	Crossleys, Halifax.
London : Falcon Hall, 15, Silver Street . . .	Crossleys Limited, London.
Manchester : 57, Portland Street	Tapestry, Manchester.
Cunard Steamship Co., Limited, Liverpool	Cunard, Liverpool.
Davey & Son, Old Barge House Wharf, Blackfriars Bridge, London	Wallsend, London.
Dawson, O. E., 10, Hart Street, Bloomsbury Square, London, W.C.	Dorart, London.
Debenham & Freebody, Wigmore Street and Welbeck Street, London	Debenham, London.
Debenham, Tewson, Farmer, & Bridgwater, 80, Cheapside, London	Debenhams, Cheapside, London.
Dickeson, Sir Richard, and Company, Victoria Warehouses, Mansell Street, London	Richard Dickeson, London.
Dover : Market Lane	Dickeson, Dover.
Dublin : Ellis's Quay	Dickeson, Dublin.
Aldershot	Dickeson, Aldershot.
Dickinson, John, & Co., 65, Old Bailey, London . .	Commiles, London.
Dinning & Cooke, Percy Iron Works, Newcastle-on-Tyne	Dinning, Newcastle-on-Tyne.
Downing, J. S., Crown Works, Commercial Street, Birmingham	Downing, Birmingham.
Dublin and Wicklow Manure Company, Limited, 1, College Street, Dublin	Dubwick, Dublin.
Dunn & Wright, Printers and Publishers, 100—102, West George Street and 100—106, Stirling Road, Glasgow .	Chardon, Glasgow.
Eason, Charles, Publisher, 13, Aston's Quay, Dublin . .	Eason, Dublin.
Eglinton Chemical Co., Limited, Irvine, N.B. . . .	Eglinton, Irvine.
Emmet, John, & Co., Springfield Paper Mills, Bolton . .	Emmet, Bolton.
English and Foreign Electrotype Agency, 19, Ludgate Hill, London, E.C.	Electragt, London.
Eyre & Spottiswoode, Great New Street, London . .	Spotless, London.
Faris, David, Warstone Lane, Birmingham . . .	Faris, Birmingham.
Faudel, Phillips & Sons, 36 to 40, Newgate Street, London	Faudel, London.
Fauvel, C. H., 4, Carlton Terrace, Southampton . .	
Feltham & Co., City Steam Works, Little Britain, London .	Felthams, London.
Fernau & Eltze, 133, West Campbell Street, Glasgow . .	Fernau, Glasgow.
Finlayson, Bousfield & Co., Flax Mills, Johnstone, N.B. .	Finlayson, Johnstone.
Fleming, F. & A. B. & Co., Limited, Chemical Works, Caroline Park, Edinburgh ; (London Office, 15, Whitefriars St.)	Caroline, Edinburgh.
Foster, Porter & Co., Limited, 47, Wood Street, London .	Fosporter, London.
Fraser & Fraser, Bromley-by-Bow, London . . .	Pressure, London.
Fulcher, Arthur, Milgate Park, Maidstone. (Telegraph Station, Bearstead)	
Gardner, Jno.; & Son, 11, Bradford Street, Birmingham .	Simplex, Birmingham.
Gillig's United States Exchange, 9, Strand, Charing Cross, London	Rendezvous, London.
Glasgow and West of Scotland Guardian Society for the Protection of Trade, 145, Queen Street, Glasgow . .	Guardian, Glasgow,
Dundee	Guardian, Dundee.
Godden, William Jefferys, Solicitor, Point Pinellas, Hillsborough County, Florida, U.S.A.	
Grand Hotel, Broad Street, Bristol	Grand, Bristol.
Grand Hotel, Trafalgar Square, London . . .	Granotel, London.

H *

NAME OF FIRM.	REGISTERED TELEGRAPHIC ADDRESS.
Grant & Co., 72 and 75, Turnmill Street London	Grants, London.
Green & Sons, Printers, Beverley	Green, Beverley.
Green, F., & Co., 13, Fenchurch Avenue, London	Thirteen, London.
Green, H. G. Egerton, King's Ford, Colchester	
Greener, W. W., St. Mary's Square, Birmingham	Greener, Birmingham.
London : 68, Haymarket	Ejector, London.
Guion & Co., 11, Rumford Street, Liverpool	Guion, Liverpool.
Haage & Schmidt, Erfurt	Hagesmit, Erfurt.
Hallett & Co., 7, St. Martin's Place, London	Olgrande, London.
Hall, J. & E., 23, St. Swithin's Lane, London	Hallford, London.
Dartford, Kent	Hallford, Dartford.
Hansard, Henry & Son, House of Commons Printing Office, 41, Parker Street, W.C.	Hansards, London.
Haslam, John, & Co., Limited, Fountain Street, Manchester	Squirrels, Manchester.
Bolton	Squirrels, Bolton.
London	Squirrels, London.
Haynes, George, & Co., Hampstead Cotton Mills, Cherry Tree Lane, Stockport	Haynes, Stockport.
Henderson Brothers, "Anchor" Line, 47, Union Street, Glasgow	Anchor, Glasgow.
Henry, A. S., & Co., Huddersfield	Henrys, Huddersfield.
Heywood, John, Publisher and Bookseller, Deansgate, Manchester	Books, Manchester.
Hildesheimer & Faulkner, 41, Jewin Street, London	Labor, London.
Hobbs, W., & Sons, Printers and Chromo-Lithographers, Maidstone	Hobbs, Maidstone.
Hogg, Alexander, & Co., 60, Virginia Street, Glasgow	Hogg, Glasgow.
Holden, Burnley & Co., Cumberland Works, Cemetery Road, Bradford	Burnley, Girlington.
Holden, George, & Son, 21, Carter Lane, Old Change, London	Holden, London.
Holden, Isaac, & Sons, Alston Works, Bradford	Holdens, Bradford.
Hooper & Co., Covent Garden, London	Hortus, London.
Horn & Son, Patent Agents, Somerset Chambers, 151, Strand, London	Wide-a-wake, London.
Hornbuckle, W. A., & Co., 18, Billiter Street, London	Hornbuckle, London.
Hôtel Métropole, Northumberland Avenue, London	Métropole, London.
Houlston & Sons, 7, Paternoster Buildings, London	Houlston, London.
Howatson, George S., 20, Bucklersbury, London	George Howatson, London.
Howell, Henry, & Co., 180, Old Street, London	Henry Howell, London.
Howell, John, & Co., Limited, 3, St. Paul's Churchyard, London	Howell, London.
Hughes, Thomas, & Co., 194, Euston Road, London	Navigable, London.
Illingworth, Daniel, & Sons, Whetley Mills, Bradford	Illingworth, Bradford.
Ismay, John, & Sons, Newcastle-on-Tyne	Ismays, Newcastle-on-Tyne.
Jarvis, J. W., & Son, 28, King William Street, Strand, London	Biblionist, London.
Jennings, George, Palace Wharf, Stangate, London	Jennings, London.
Johnson, Matthey & Co., 78, Hatton Garden, London	Matthey, London.
Johnson, Walker & Tolhurst, 80, Aldersgate Street, London	Jowato, London.
Johnston, W. and A. K., 5, White Hart Street, Warwick Lane, London	Geographers, London.

NAME OF FIRM.	REGISTERED TELEGRAPHIC ADDRESS.
Junior Army and Navy Stores, Limited :—	
London : York House, Waterloo Place . . .	Supplies, London.
Aldershot : 16, 17, and 18, Union Street . . .	Supplies, Aldershot.
Dublin : 22, 23, and 24, D'Olier Street . . .	Supplies, Dublin.
Keen, Robinson & Bellville, Garlick Hill, Cannon Street, London }	Keen, London.
Kerr & Richardson, Wholesale Stationers, 89, Queen Street, Glasgow . . . . }	Ellisland, Glasgow.
Keyser, A., & Co., Foreign Bankers, 21, Cornhill, London :—	
For Inland telegrams	Keyser, Cornhill, London.
For Foreign and Colonial telegrams . . .	Keyser, London.
Kiddier, J., & Son, Globe Works, Waterway Street, Nottingham	Kiddier, Nottingham.
Kirby, Beard & Co., 115, Newgate Street, London .	Ravenhurst, London.
Lang & Co., 146 and 150, Ingram Street, Glasgow .	Langkelty, Glasgow.
London : 16, Watling Street	Langkelty, London.
Leadbeater & Scott, St. Mary's Works, Peniston Road, Sheffield }	Leadbeater, Sheffield.
Leaf, Sons & Co., Old Change, London . . .	Leaf, London.
Leckie, John, & Co., Walsall	Leckie, Walsall.
London : 12, St. Mary Axe . . .	Saddlery, London.
Legbrannock District Collieries Company, Limited, 21, Hope Street, near Central Station, Glasgow . . }	Waldie, Glasgow.
Leisler, Bock, & Co., Glasgow	Leisler, Glasgow.
Leith Distillery, Leith	Bernard, Leith.
Lepard & Smiths, 29, King Street, Covent Garden, London }	Lepard, London.
Leslie, D., Wholesale Stationer, Perth . . .	Leslie, Perth.
Letts, Charles, & Co., 3, Royal Exchange, London .	Diarists, London.
Lilleshall Company, Limited, Priors Lee Hall, near Shifnal	Lilleshall, Oakengates.
Lindley, C., & Co., 34, Englefield Road, London . .	Beauvoir, London.
Linklater & Niven, Queen's Chambers, Pirie Street, Adelaide, South Australia . . . . }	Haddon, Adelaide.
Lister & Co., Manningham Mills, Bradford . .	Lister, Bradford.
Little, John, The Library, Wrexham . . .	Little, Wrexham.
Lockwood (Crosby) & Co., 7, Stationers' Hall Court, Ludgate Hill, London . . . . }	Crosblock, London.
London Mercantile Association, Limited, 8, Finch Lane, London . . . . }	Mercable.
Lotz, Abbott & Co., 66, Queen Street, London . .	Ingbooth, London.
Maclure & Macdonald, 2, Bothwell Circus, Glasgow .	Lithographers, Glasgow.
Macmuldrow, Peter, Steam Saw Mills, London Road, Liverpool . . . . }	Macmuldrow, Liverpool.
Macniven & Wallace, 132, Princes Street, Edinburgh .	Library, Edinburgh.
Maconochie Brothers, Lowestoft	Maconochie, Lowestoft.
London : 1, East India Avenue . . .	Maconochie, London.
Malton Gas Company, Gas Works, Malton . . .	Gas, Malton.
Mardon, Son & Hall, The Caxton Works, Bristol .	Mardon's, Bristol.
Marlborough, E., & Co., 51, Old Bailey, London .	} Marlborough, London.
Marlborough, Gould & Co., 52, Old Bailey, London .	
Marquess of Ailsa	Ailsa, Maybole.
Marriott, H. & F. A., Birstall, near Leeds . . .	Marriott, Birstall.
Marshall Brothers, 3, Amen Corner, Paternoster Row, London . . . . }	Grapho, London.

NAME OF FIRM.	REGISTERED TELEGRAPHIC ADDRESS.
Mawson, Swan & Morgan, Stationers, &c., Newcastle-on-Tyne .	Morgan, Newcastle-on-Tyne.
Merry & Cuninghame, 127, St. Vincent Street, Glasgow .	Merry, Glasgow.
Meux & Co., Limited, Horse Shoe Brewery, London .	Meuxs, London.
Midland Educational Company, Limited, 91 and 92, New Street, Birmingham .	Educational, Birmingham.
Midland Grand Hotel, St. Pancras Station, London .	Midotel, London.
Millington & Sons, 32, Budge Row, London .	Millington, London.
Montagu, Samuel, & Co., 60, Old Broad Street, London	Montagu, London.
Morris & Griffin, Ceres Works, Wolverhampton .	Ceres, Wolverhampton.
Newport, Monmouth .	Fuller, Maindee, Mon.
Morrison & Gibb, 11, Queen Street, Edinburgh .	Magazine, Edinburgh.
Mort, Liddell & Co., Widnes .	Mort, Widnes.
Mortimer, Edward, Bookseller and Printer, Halifax .	Mortimer, Halifax.
Motherwell, R., & Co., 43, Queen Street, Glasgow .	Motherwell, Glasgow.
Mowbray, A. R., & Co., 1186, St. Aldate's, Oxford	Mowbray, Oxford.
London : 65, Farringdon Street .	Anglicanus, London.
Nettlefold & Sons, 54, High Holborn, London .	Nettleson, London.
Newton, Chambers & Co., Limited, Thorncliffe Iron Works and Collieries, near Sheffield .	Newton, Sheffield.
Normandy, A. Stilwell, & Co., Victoria Docks, London .	Normandy, London.
Northcote, Stafford, & Co., St. Paul's Churchyard, London .	Stafford Northcote, London.
North of England School Furnishing Co., Limited, 25, Grainger Street West, Newcastle-on-Tyne .	Scholastic, Newcastle-on-Tyne.
Novelli & Co., Billiter House, Billiter Street, London .	Novelli, London.
Ocean and Continental Express, 35, Haymarket, London .	Nixon, London.
Oetzmann & Co., 67 to 79, Hampstead Road, London	Oetzmann, London.
Ogilvie & Moore, Warren's Place, Cork .	Ogilvie, Cork.
Orient Steam Navigation Co., Limited, 13, Fenchurch Avenue, London .	Orient, London.
Page & Sandeman, 5½, Pall Mall, London .	Torniport, London.
Pantin, W. & C., 147, Upper Thames Street, London .	Pantinko.
Partridge, S. W., & Co., 9, Paternoster Row, London .	Pictorial, London.
Paul (Kegan), Trench & Co., 1, Paternoster Square, London	Columnae, London.
Pawson & Co., Limited, St. Paul's Churchyard, London .	Pawson, London.
Peake, Thomas, The Tileries, Tunstall, Staffordshire .	Peake, Tunstall, Staff.
Philip, Son & Nephew, 51, South Castle Street, Liverpool .	Education, Liverpool.
Pigou, Wilks & Laurence, Limited, 11, Queen Victoria Street, London	Pigou, London.
Pirie, Alex., & Sons, Limited, Stoneywood Works, Auchmill, Aberdeenshire	Pirie, Aberdeen.
Pitman, Frederick, 20 and 21, Paternoster Row, London .	Pitman, London.
Pitt & Scott, Foreign Parcels Express :—	
London : 23, Cannon Street	Pitt Scott, London.
Liverpool : Corf's Buildings, 16, Preeson's Row .	Pitt Scott, Liverpool.
Paris : 7, Rue Scribe .	Pitt, Paris.
Poole, Henry, & Co., 36 to 39, Savile Row, London .	Eloop, London.
Porteous, James & Son, 5, Dixon Street, Glasgow .	Porteous, Glasgow.
Poulten, Thomas, & Sons, 6, Arthur Street West, London Bridge, London .	Poulter, London.
Price, R. J. Lloyd, 10, Wilton Crescent, London .	Canis, London.
Rhiwlas, Bala, North Wales .	Price, Bala.

NAME OF FIRM.	REGISTERED TELEGRAPHIC ADDRESS.
Price, Sons, & Co., Bristol	Price, Bristol.
Pullman Company, Limited, St. Pancras Station, London	Pullman, London.
Pullman, R. & J., 17, Greek Street, Soho, London	Leathersellers, London.
Religious Tract and Book Society of Scotland, Edinburgh	Tract Society, Edinburgh.
Remington & Co., 18, Henrietta Street, Covent Garden, London	Proficio, London.
Richardson & Chadbaum, 8, Finch Lane, London	Mercable, London.
Royal Mail Steam Packet Co., 18, Moorgate Street, London	Omarius, London.
Rylands & Sons, Limited, New High Street, Manchester	Rylands, Manchester.
Samuel & Escombe, 26, Austin Friars, E.C.	Gainsay, London.
Selwood Printing Works, Frome	Selwood, Frome.
Shelton Iron & Steel Company, Limited, Stoke-upon-Trent, Staffordshire	Shelton, Stoke-on-Trent.
London Offices : 122, Cannon Street, E.C.	Sheltonian, London.
Sherwill, J. H., Market Street, Devonport	Sherwill, Grocer, Devonport.
Siemens Brothers & Co., Limited, 12, Queen Anne's Gate, London	Siemens, London.
Silverlock, Henry, 92, Blackfriars Road, London	Silverlock, London.
Smith & Ebbs, Northumberland Buildings, Fenchurch Street, London	Adept, London.
Smith, W. H., & Son, 80, Middle Abbey Street, Dublin	Season, Dublin.
Sotheran, Henry, & Co., 136, Strand, London	Bookmen, London.
London : 36, Piccadilly	
Manchester : 49, Cross Street	Bookmen, Manchester.
Squire & Sons, 413, Oxford Street, London	Squire, London.
Stanhope Company, Limited, 20, Bucklersbury, London	Stanhope, London.
Stapley & Smith, London Wall, London	Stapley, London.
Star Brush Company, The, Eden Grove, Holloway, N.	Stellatus, London.
Starkey, R. W., & Son, 27, New Bridge Street, Blackfriars, London	Starkey, London.
Steel Company of Scotland, Limited, 150, Hope Street, Glasgow	Steel, Glasgow.
Stone, Henry, & Son, Box Manufactory, Banbury	Stone, Banbury.
Stubbs' Mercantile Offices, 42, Gresham Street, London	Stubbs, London.
Summerlee & Mossend Iron & Steel Company, Limited, 172, West George Street, Glasgow	Summerlee, Glasgow.
Swiss, A. H., Bookseller and Printer, Devonport	Alfred Swiss, Devonport.
Tate, Henry, & Sons :—	
London : 21, Mincing Lane	Tateson, London.
Silvertown : Thames Sugar Refinery	Tate, Silvertown.
Liverpool : 15H, Exchange Buildings	Tateson, Liverpool.
Terrell, William, & Sons, Limited, Welsh Back, Bristol	Terrell, Bristol.
Tharsis Sulphur and Copper Co., Limited, 136, West George Street, Glasgow	Tharsis, Glasgow.
Thomson, Henry, & Co., Newry	Thomson, Newry.
Thomson & Campbell, 5, Adelphi Terrace, Strand	Yacht, London.
Tuck, Raphael, & Sons, 72 and 73, Coleman Street, London	Palette, London.
Union Steamship Company, Limited, 11, Leadenhall Street, London	Oregon, London.
United Asbestos Co., Limited, 161, Queen Victoria Street, London	Asbestos, London.
Unwin, Robert, & Co., 1, Old Hall Street, Liverpool	Silverstone, Liverpool.
Vicars, T. and T., Seel Street, Liverpool	Outters, Liverpool.
London : 20, Bucklersbury	George Howatson, London.

NAME OF FIRM.	REGISTERED TELEGRAPHIC ADDRESS.
Vulcan Iron Works, Langley Mill, near Nottingham . .	Turner, Langley Mill.
Walch & Butler, Solicitors, Hobart, Tasmania . . .	Vibex, Hobart.
Walker, Howard & Co., 70, Lower Thames Street, London .	Evering, London.
Walker, John, & Co., Farringdon House, Warwick Lane, London	Chebucto, London.
Waterlow & Sons, Limited, London Wall, London . .	Waterlow Sons, London.
Waterston, George, & Sons, 56, Hanover Street, Edinburgh	Waterstons, Edinburgh.
London : 9, Rose Street, Newgate Street . . .	Waterstons, London.
Watson & Co., G. L., 108, West Regent Street, Glasgow .	Vril, Glasgow.
Wells, A., & Co., Steam Works, Spanish Road, Wandsworth, London	Tinkery, London.
Werner & Pfleiderer, 86, Upper Ground Street, Blackfriars Bridge, London	Pfleiderer, London.
White, John, 26, Great St. Helens, London	John White, London.
White, Robert Stanley, Solicitor, 12, New Inn, Strand, London, W.C.; and Queen Anne's Lodge, Lordship Road, Stoke Newington.	
Widnes Alkali Co., Limited, Widnes	Widnes, Widnes.
Liverpool : 1 and 2, Bank Buildings, 60, Castle Street	Soda, Liverpool.
Williams, J. D., & Co., Langley Mills Manufacturing Co., Manchester	Witches, Manchester.
Wilmott, Edward W., Passenger Shipping Agent, Malta .	Wilmott, Malta.
Winn & Holland, Montreal	Winn, Montreal.
Wood & Ingram, The Nurseries, Huntingdon . . .	Ingram, Huntingdon.
Wood's Hotel, Furnival's Inn, London	Woodsdon, London.
Woodward, Clark, & Co., Nottingham	Woodward, Nottingham.
Worthington & Co., Brewers, Burton	Worthingtons, Burton.
Wright, Layman, & Umney, 50, Southwark Street, London	Umney, London.
Wrigley, James, & Son, Limited:—	
London : 21, Budge Row	Wrigleys, London.
Bury	Wrigleys, Bury.
Manchester	Wandson, Manchester.

PRINTED BY CASSELL & COMPANY, LIMITED, LA BELLE SAUVAGE, LONDON, E.C.

10.1080

Illustrated, Fine Art, and other Volumes.

Abbeys and Churches of England and Wales, The: Descriptive, Historical, Pictorial. 21s.

Adventure, The World of. Fully Illustrated. 9s.

After London; or, Wild England. By RICHARD JEFFERIES. *Cheap Edition.* 3s. 6d.

Along Alaska's Great River. By Lieut. SCHWATKA. Illustrated. 12s. 6d.

American Academy Notes. Illustrated Art Notes upon the National Academy of Design, 1889. 2s. 6d.

American Yachts and Yachting. Illustrated. 6s.

Animal Painting in Water Colours. With Eighteen Coloured Plates by FREDERICK TAYLER. 5s.

Arabian Nights Entertainments (Cassell's). With about 400 Illustrations. 10s. 6d.

Architectural Drawing. By PHENÉ SPIERS. Illustrated. 10s. 6d.

Art, The Magazine of. Yearly Volume. With several hundred Engravings, and Twelve Etchings, Photogravures, &c. Vol. for 1889, 16s.

Behind Time. By G. P. LATHROP. Illustrated. 2s. 6d.

Bismarck, Prince. By C. LOWE, M.A. Two Vols. *Cheap Edition.* 10s. 6d.

Black Arrow, The. A Tale of the Two Roses. By R. L. STEVENSON. 5s.

British Ballads. 275 Original Illustrations. Two Vols. Cloth, 7s. 6d. each.

British Battles on Land and Sea. By JAMES GRANT. With about 600 Illustrations. Three Vols., 4to, £1 7s.; Library Edition, £1 10s.

British Battles, Recent. Illustrated. 4to, 9s. Library Edition, 10s.

British Empire, The. By SIR GEORGE CAMPBELL. 3s.

British Museum, The Bible Student in the. By the Rev. J. G. KITCHIN, M.A. Fcap. 8vo, 1s.

Browning, An Introduction to the Study of. By ARTHUR SYMONS. 2s. 6d.

Butterflies and Moths, European. By W. F. KIRBY. With 61 Coloured Plates. Demy 4to, 35s.

Canaries and Cage-Birds, The Illustrated Book of. By W. A. BLAKSTON, W. SWAYSLAND, and A. F. WIENER. With 56 Fac-simile Coloured Plates, 35s.

Cannibals and Convicts. By JULIAN THOMAS ("The Vagabond"). *Cheap Edition,* 5s.

Captain Trafalgar. By WESTALL and LAURIE. Illustrated. 5s.

Cassell's Family Magazine. Yearly Vol. Illustrated. 9s.

Cathedral Churches of England and Wales. Descriptive, Historical, Pictorial. *Édition de luxe.* Roxburgh, 42s.

Celebrities of the Century: Being a Dictionary of Men and Women of the Nineteenth Century. 21s.; roxburgh, 25s.

Changing Year, The. With Illustrations. 7s. 6d.

Chess Problem, The. With Illustrations by C. PLANCK and others. 7s. 6d.

Children of the Cold, The. By Lieut. SCHWATKA. 2s. 6d.

China Painting. By FLORENCE LEWIS. With Sixteen Coloured Plates, and a selection of Wood Engravings. With full Instructions. 5s.

Choice Dishes at Small Cost. By A. G. PAYNE. *Cheap Edition,* 1s.

Christmas in the Olden Time. By Sir WALTER SCOTT. With charming Original Illustrations. 7s. 6d.

Cities of the World. Four Vols. Illustrated. 7s. 6d. each.

Civil Service, Guide to Employment in the. *New and Enlarged Edition.* 3s. 6d.

Civil Service.—Guide to Female Employment in Government Offices. Cloth, 1s.

Clinical Manuals for Practitioners and Students of Medicine. (*A List of Volumes forwarded post free on application to the Publishers.*)

Clothing, The Influence of, on Health. By FREDERICK TREVES, F.R.C.S. 2s.

Cobden Club, Some Works published for the. (*A Complete List post free on application*):—

Colour. By Prof. A. H. CHURCH. *New and Enlarged Edition.* 3s. 6d.

Columbus, Christopher, The Life and Voyages of. By WASHINGTON IRVING. Three Vols. 7s. 6d.

Commerce, The Year Book of. Edited by KENRIC B. MURRAY. 5s.

Commodore Junk. By G. MANVILLE FENN. 5s.

Cook Book, Catherine Owen's New. 4s.

Cookery, A Year's. By PHYLLIS BROWNE. Cloth gilt or oiled cloth, 3s. 6d.

Cookery, Cassell's Dictionary of. Containing about Nine Thousand Recipes. 7s. 6d. ; roxburgh, 10s. 6d.

Cookery, Cassell's Shilling. *40th Thousand.* 1s.

Countries of the World, The. By ROBERT BROWN, M.A., Ph.D., &c. Complete in Six Vols., with about 750 Illustrations. 4to, 7s. 6d. each.

Cremation and Urn-Burial; or, The Cemeteries of the Future. By W. ROBINSON. With Plates and Illustrations. 1s.

Cromwell, Oliver: The Man and His Mission. By J. ALLANSON PICTON, M.P. *Cheap Edition.* With Steel Portrait. 5s.

Culmshire Folk. By the Author of "John Orlebar," &c. 3s. 6d.

Cyclopædia, Cassell's Concise. With 12,000 subjects, brought down to the latest date. With about 600 Illustrations, 15s. ; roxburgh, 18s.

Cyclopædia, Cassell's Miniature. Containing 30,000 Subjects. Cloth, 3s. 6d.

Dairy Farming. By Prof. J. P. SHELDON. With 25 Fac-simile Coloured Plates, and numerous Wood Engravings. Demy 4to, 21s.

Dead Man's Rock. A Romance. By Q. 5s.

Dickens, Character Sketches from. FIRST, SECOND, and THIRD SERIES. With Six Original Drawings in each, by FREDERICK BARNARD. In Portfolio, 21s. each.

Dog, Illustrated Book of the. By VERO SHAW, B.A. With 28 Coloured Plates. Cloth bevelled, 35s. ; half-morocco, 45s.

Dog Stories and Dog Lore. By Col. THOS. W. KNOX. 6s.

Dog, The. By IDSTONE. Illustrated. 2s. 6d.

Domestic Dictionary, The. An Encyclopædia for the Household. Cloth, 7s. 6d.

Doré Gallery, The. With 250 Illustrations by GUSTAVE DORÉ. 4to, 42s.

Doré's Dante's Inferno. Illustrated by GUSTAVE DORÉ. *Popular Edition*, 21s.

Doré's Dante's Purgatorio and Paradiso. Illustrated by GUSTAVE DORÉ. *Popular Edition.* 21s.

Doré's Fairy Tales Told Again. With 24 Full-page Engravings by DORÉ. 5s.

Doré's Milton's Paradise Lost. Illustrated by GUSTAVE DORÉ. 4to, 21s.

Earth, Our, and its Story. By Dr. ROBERT BROWN, F.L.S. With Coloured Plates and numerous Wood Engravings. Vols. I. and II. 9s. each.

Edinburgh, Old and New, Cassell's. With 600 Illustrations. Three Vols., 9s. each ; library binding, £1 10s. the set.

Egypt: Descriptive, Historical, and Picturesque. By Prof. G. EBERS. Translated by CLARA BELL, with Notes by SAMUEL BIRCH, LL.D., &c. *Popular Edition*, in Two Vols., 42s.

"89." A Novel. By EDGAR HENRY. Cloth, 3s. 6d.

Electricity, Age of, from Amber Soul to Telephone. By PARK BENJAMIN, Ph.D. 7s. 6d.

Electricity, Practical. By Prof. W. E. AYRTON. Illustrated. 7s. 6d.

Encyclopædic Dictionary, The. A New and Original Work of Reference to all the Words in the English Language. Complete in Fourteen Divisional Vols., 10s. 6d. each ; or Seven Vols., half-morocco, 21s. each ; half-russia, 25s. each.

Engineering, Triumphs of. By HENRY FRITH. With Eight Full-page Illustrations. 5s.

England, Cassell's Illustrated History of. With 2,000 Illustrations. Ten Vols., 4to, 9s. each. *New and Revised Edition.* Vols. I., II., and III., 9s. each.

English History, The Dictionary of. *Cheap Edition,* 10s. 6d.

English Literature, Library of. By Prof. HENRY MORLEY. Complete in 5 vols., 7s. 6d. each.

VOL. I.—SHORTER ENGLISH POEMS.	VOL. IV.—SHORTER WORKS IN ENGLISH PROSE.
VOL. II.—ILLUSTRATIONS OF ENGLISH RELIGION.	VOL. V.—SKETCHES OF LONGER WORKS IN ENGLISH VERSE AND PROSE.
VOL. III.—ENGLISH PLAYS.	

English Literature, Morley's First Sketch of. *Revised Edition,* 7s. 6d.

English Literature, The Dictionary of. By W. DAVENPORT ADAMS. *Cheap Edition,* 7s. 6d. ; roxburgh, 10s. 6d.

English Literature, The Story of. By ANNA BUCKLAND. *New and Cheap Edition.* 3s. 6d.

English Writers. An attempt towards a History of English Literature. By HENRY MORLEY, LL.D., Professor of English Literature, University College, London. Vols. I., II., III., IV., and V., 5s. each.

Æsop's Fables. With about 150 Illustrations by E. GRISET. *Cheap Edition,* cloth, 3s. 6d. ; bevelled boards, gilt edges, 5s.

Etching : Its Technical Processes, with Remarks on Collections and Collecting. By S. K. KOEHLER. Illustrated with 30 Full-page Plates. Price £4 4s.

Etiquette of Good Society. 1s. ; cloth, 1s. 6d.

Eye, Ear, and Throat, The Management of the. 3s. 6d.

Family Physician, The. By Eminent PHYSICIANS and SURGEONS. *New and Revised Edition.* Cloth, 21s. ; roxburgh, 25s.

Fenn, G. Manville, Works by. *Popular Editions.* Boards, 2s. each ; or cloth, 2s. 6d.

Dutch the Diver; or, a Man's Mistake.	Poverty Corner.
My Patients.	The Vicar's People. } In Cloth only.
The Parson o' Dumford.	Sweet Mace.

Ferns, European. By JAMES BRITTEN, F.L.S. With 30 Fac-simile Coloured Plates by D. BLAIR, F.L.S. 21s.

Field Naturalist's Handbook, The. By Rev. J. G. WOOD & THEODORE WOOD. 5s.

Figuier's Popular Scientific Works. With Several Hundred Illustrations in each. 3s. 6d. each.

The Human Race.	The Ocean World.
World Before the Deluge.	The Vegetable World.
Reptiles and Birds.	The Insect World.
Mammalia.	

Figure Painting in Water Colours. With 16 Coloured Plates by BLANCHE MACARTHUR and JENNIE MOORE. With full Instructions. 7s. 6d.

Fine-Art Library, The. Edited by JOHN SPARKES, Principal of the South Kensington Art Schools. Each Book contains about 100 Illustrations. 5s. each.

Tapestry. By Eugène Müntz. Translated by Miss L. J. Davis.	The Education of the Artist. By Ernest Chesneau. Translated by Clara Bell. Non-illustrated.
Engraving. By Le Vicomte Henri Delaborde. Translated by R. A. M. Stevenson.	Greek Archæology. By Maxime Collignon. Translated by Dr. J. H. Wright.
The English School of Painting. By E. Chesneau. Translated by L. N. Etherington. With an Introduction by Prof. Ruskin.	Artistic Anatomy. By Prof. Duval. Translated by F. E. Fenton.
The Flemish School of Painting. By A. J. Wauters. Translated by Mrs. Henry Rossel.	The Dutch School of Painting. By Henry Havard. Translated by G. Powell.

Flora's Feast: a Masque of Flowers. With Coloured Designs by WALTER CRANE. 5s.

Flower Painting, Elementary. With Eight Coloured Plates. 3s.

Flower Painting in Water Colours. With Coloured Plates. First and Second Series. 5s. each.

Flower Painting in Water Colours. First and Second Series. With 20 Fac-simile Coloured Plates in each by F. E. HULME, F.L.S., F.S.A. With Instructions by the Artist. Interleaved. 5s. each.

Flowers, and How to Paint Them. By MAUD NAFTEL. With Coloured Plates. 5s.

Forging of the Anchor, The. A Poem. By Sir SAMUEL FERGUSON, LL.D. With 20 Original Illustrations. Gilt edges, 5s.

Fossil Reptiles, A History of British. By Sir RICHARD OWEN, K.C.B., F.R.S., &c. With 268 Plates. In Four Vols., £12 12s.

France as It Is. By ANDRÉ LEBON and PAUL PELET. With Three Maps. Crown 8vo. cloth, 7s. 6d.

Franco-German War, Cassell's History of the. Two Vols. With 500 Illustrations. 9s. each.

Fresh-Water Fishes of Europe, The. By Prof. H. G. SEELEY, F.R.S. *Cheap Edition.* 7s. 6d.

Garden Flowers, Familiar. By SHIRLEY HIBBERD. With Coloured Plates by F. E. HULME, F.L.S. Complete in Five Series. Cloth gilt, 12s. 6d. each.

Gardening, Cassell's Popular. Illustrated. Complete in 4 Vols., 5s. each.

Geometrical Drawing for Army Candidates. By H. T. LILLEY, M.A. 2s.

Geometry, First Elements of Experimental. By PAUL BERT. 1s. 6d.

Geometry, Practical Solid. By Major ROSS. 2s.

Germany, Emperor William of. By ARCHIBALD FORBES. 3s. 6d.

Gladstone, Life of the Rt. Hon. W. E. By G. BARNETT SMITH. With Portrait. 3s. 6d.

Gleanings from Popular Authors. Two Vols. With Original Illustrations. 4to, 9s. each. Two Vols. in One, 15s.

Great Northern Railway, The Official Illustrated Guide to the. 1s.; cloth, 2s.

Great Painters of Christendom, The, from Cimabue to Wilkie. By JOHN FORBES-ROBERTSON. Illustrated throughout. *Popular Edition,* cloth gilt, 12s. 6d.

Great Western Railway, The Official Illustrated Guide to the. *New and Revised Edition.* 1s.; cloth, 2s.

Gulliver's Travels. With 88 Engravings by MORTEN. *Cheap Edition.* Cloth, 3s. 6d.; cloth gilt, 5s.

Gum Boughs and Wattle Bloom. By DONALD MACDONALD. 5s.

Gun and its Development, The. By W. W. GREENER. Illustrated. 10s. 6d.

Guns, Modern Shot. By W. W. GREENER. Illustrated. 5s.

Gunmaker of Moscow, The. A Novel. By SYLVANUS COBB, Junr. Cloth, 3s. 6d.

Health at School. By CLEMENT DUKES, M.D., B.S. 7s. 6d. [burgh, 25s.

Health, The Book of. By Eminent Physicians and Surgeons. Cloth, 21s.; rox-

Health, The Influence of Clothing on. By F. TREVES, F.R.C.S. 2s.

Heavens, The Story of the. By Sir ROBERT STAWELL BALL, LL.D., F.R.S., Royal Astronomer of Ireland. Coloured Plates and Wood Engravings. 31s. 6d.

Heroes of Britain in Peace and War. In Two Vols., with 300 Original Illustrations. 5s. each; or One Vol., library binding, 10s. 6d.

Holy Land and the Bible, The. By the Rev. CUNNINGHAM GEIKIE, D.D. With Map. Two Vols. 24s.

Homes, Our, and How to Make them Healthy. By Eminent Authorities. Illustrated. 15s.; roxburgh, 18s.

Horse, The Book of the. By SAMUEL SIDNEY. With 28 Fac-simile Coloured Plates. Demy 4to, 35s.; half-morocco, £2 5s.

Household, Cassell's Book of the. Illustrated. Vol. I. 5s.

Household Guide, Cassell's. With Illustrations and Coloured Plates. *New and Revised Edition,* complete in Four Vols., 20s.

How Dante Climbed the Mountain. By ROSE EMILY SELFE. With Eight Full-page Engravings by GUSTAVE DORÉ. 2s.

How Women may Earn a Living. By MERCY GROGAN. *Cheap Edition.* 6d.

India, Cassell's History of. By JAMES GRANT. With 400 Illustrations. 15s.

In-door Amusements, Card Games, and Fireside Fun, Cassell's. 3s. 6d.

Industrial Remuneration Conference. The Report of. 2s. 6d.

Insect Variety: its Propagation and Distribution. By A. H. SWINTON. 7s. 6d.

Irish Parliament, A Miniature History of the. By J. C. HASLAM. 3d.

Irish Parliament, The: What it Was, and What it Did. By J. G. SWIFT McNEILL, M.A., M.P. 1s.

Irish Question, The Speaker's Hand-book on the. By an IRISH LIBERAL. 1s.

Irish Union, The: Before and After. By A. K. CONNELL, M.A. 2s. 6d.

John Parmelee's Curse. By JULIAN HAWTHORNE. 2s. 6d.

Karmel the Scout. A Novel. By SYLVANUS COBB, Junr. Cloth, 3s. 6d.

Kennel Guide, Practical. By Dr. GORDON STABLES. Illustrated. *Cheap Edition.* 1s.

Khiva, A Ride to. By Col. FRED BURNABY. 1s. 6d.

Kidnapped. By R. L. STEVENSON. *Illustrated Edition.* 5s.

King Solomon's Mines. By H. RIDER HAGGARD. *Illustrated Edition.* 5s.

Ladies' Physician, The. By a London Physician. 6s.

Lady Biddy Fane, The Admirable. By FRANK BARRETT. *Popular Edition,* crown 8vo 5s.; Three Vols., Cloth, 31s. 6d.

Landscape Painting in Oils, A Course of Lessons in. By A. F. GRACE. With Nine Reproductions in Colour. *Cheap Edition,* 25s.

Law, How to Avoid. By A. J. WILLIAMS, M.P. *Cheap Edition.* 1s.

Laws of Every Day Life, The. By H. O. ARNOLD-FORSTER. 1s. 6d. *Presentation Edition.* 3s. 6d.

Legends for Lionel. By WALTER CRANE. Coloured Illustrations. 5s.

Letts's Diaries and other Time-saving Publications are now published exclusively by CASSELL & COMPANY. (*A List sent post free on application.*)

Life of Henry Richard, M.P. By CHARLES MIALL. With Portrait. 7s. 6d.

Local Government in England and Germany. By the Rt. Hon. Sir ROBERT MORIER, G.C.B., &c. 1s.

London and North Western Railway, The Official Illustrated Guide to the. 1s. ; cloth, 2s.

London and South Western Railway, The Official Illustrated Guide to the. 1s. ; cloth, 2s.

London, Brighton and South Coast Railway, The Official Illustrated Guide to the. 1s. ; cloth, 2s.

London (Ancient and Modern). From the Sanitary and Medical Point of View. By G. V. POORE, M.D., F.R.C.P. Illustrated. 5s.

London, Greater. By EDWARD WALFORD. Two Vols. With about 400 Illustrations. 9s. each. *Library Edition.* Two Vols. £1 the set.

London, Old and New. By WALTER THORNBURY and EDWARD WALFORD. Six Vols., each containing about 200 Illustrations and Maps. Cloth, 9s. each. *Library Edition.* Imitation roxburgh, £3.

Longfellow, H. W., Choice Poems by. Illustrated by his Son, ERNEST W. LONGFELLOW. 6s.

Longfellow's Poetical Works. *Fine-Art Edition.* Illustrated throughout with Original Engravings. Royal 4to, cloth gilt, £3 3s. *Popular Edition.* 16s.

Master of Ballantrae, The. By ROBERT LOUIS STEVENSON. 5s.

Mechanics, The Practical Dictionary of. Containing 15,000 Drawings. Four Vols. 21s. each.

Medical Handbook of Life Assurance. By JAMES EDWARD POLLOCK, M.D., F.R.C.P., and JAMES CHISHOLM, Fellow of the Institute of Actuaries, London. 7s. 6d.

Medicine, Manuals for Students of. (*A List forwarded post free on application.*)

Metropolitan Year-Book, The. Paper, 2s. ; cloth, 2s. 6d.

Midland Railway, The Official Illustrated Guide to the. 1s. ; cloth, 2s.

Milton's L'Allegro and Il Penseroso. Fully Illustrated. Cloth, 2s. 6d.

Modern Europe, A History of. By C. A. FYFFE, M.A. 3 Vols., 12s. each.

Music, Illustrated History of. By EMIL NAUMANN. Edited by the Rev. Sir F. A. GORE OUSELEY, Bart. Illustrated. Two Vols. 31s. 6d.

National Library, Cassell's. In Weekly Volumes, each containing about 192 pages. Paper covers, 3d. ; cloth, 6d. (*A List of the Volumes already published will be sent post free on application.*)

Natural History, Cassell's Concise. By E. PERCEVAL WRIGHT, M.A., M.D., F.L.S. With several Hundred Illustrations. 7s. 6d. ; roxburgh, 10s. 6d.

Natural History, Cassell's New. Edited by Prof. P. MARTIN DUNCAN, M.B., F.R.S., F.G.S. With Contributions by Eminent Scientific Writers. Complete in Six Vols. With about 2,000 high-class Illustrations. Extra crown 4to, cloth, 9s. each.

Nature, Short Studies from. Illustrated. *Cheap Edition.* 2s. 6d.

Nursing for the Home and for the Hospital, A Handbook of. By CATHERINE J. WOOD. *Cheap Edition.* 1s. 6d. ; cloth, 2s.

Nursing of Sick Children, A Handbook for the. By CATHERINE J. WOOD. 2s. 6d.

Orion the Gold Beater. A Novel. By SYLVANUS COBB, Junr. Cloth, 3s. 6d.

Our Own Country. Six Vols. With 1,200 Illustrations. Cloth, 7s. 6d. each.

Paxton's Flower Garden. Three Vols. With 100 Coloured Plates. £1 1s. each.

People I've Smiled With. Recollections of a Merry Little Life. By MARSHALL P. WILDER. 2s.

Peoples of the World, The. By Dr. ROBERT BROWN. Complete in Six Volumes. With Illustrations. 7s. 6d. each.

Phantom City, The. By W. WESTALL. 5s.

Photography for Amateurs. By T. C. HEPWORTH. Illustrated, 1s. ; or cloth, 1s. 6d.

Phrase and Fable, Dictionary of. By the Rev. Dr. BREWER. *Cheap Edition.* Enlarged, cloth, 3s. 6d. ; or with leather back, 4s. 6d.

Picturesque America. Complete in Four Vols., with 48 Exquisite Steel Plates, and about 800 Original Wood Engravings. £2 2s. each.

Picturesque Canada. With about 600 Original Illustrations. Two Vols., £3 3s. each.

Picturesque Europe. Complete in Five Vols. Each containing 13 Exquisite Steel Plates, from Original Drawings, and nearly 200 Original Illustrations. £2 1s. ; half-morocco, £31 10s. ; morocco gilt, £52 10s. The POPULAR EDITION is now complete in Five Vols., 18s. each.

Pigeon Keeper, The Practical. By LEWIS WRIGHT. Illustrated. 3s. 6d.

Pigeons, The Book of. By ROBERT FULTON. Edited by LEWIS WRIGHT. With 50 Coloured Plates and numerous Wood Engravings. 31s. 6d. ; half-morocco, £2 2s.

Pocket Guide to Europe (Cassell's). Size 5½ in. x 3¾ in. Leather, 6s.

Poems, Representative of Living Poets, American and English. Selected by the Poets themselves. 15s.

Poets, Cassell's Miniature Library of the :—

Burns. Two Vols. Cloth, 1s. each ; or cloth, gilt edges, 2s. 6d. the set.	**Milton.** Two Vols. Cloth, 1s. each ; or cloth, gilt edges, 2s. 6d. the set.
Byron. Two Vols. Cloth, 1s. each ; or cloth, gilt edges, 2s. 6d. the set.	**Scott.** Two Vols. Cloth, 1s. each ; or cloth, gilt edges, 2s. 6d. the set.
Hood. Two Vols. Cloth, 1s. each ; or cloth, gilt edges, 2s. 6d. the set.	**Sheridan and Goldsmith.** 2 Vols. Cloth, 1s. each ; or cloth, gilt edges, 2s. 6d. the set.
Longfellow. Two Vols. Cloth, 1s. each ; or cloth, gilt edges, 2s. 6d. the set.	**Wordsworth.** Two Vols. Cloth, 1s. each ; or cloth, gilt edges, 2s. 6d. the set.

Shakespeare. Twelve Vols., half cloth, in box, 12s.

Poor Relief in Foreign Countries, &c. By LOUISA TWINING. 1s.

Popular Library, Cassell's. A Series of New and Original Works. Cloth, 1s. each.

The Russian Empire.	John Wesley.
The Religious Revolution in the Sixteenth Century.	The Story of the English Jacobins.
English Journalism.	Domestic Folk Lore.
Our Colonial Empire.	The Rev. Rowland Hill
The Young Man in the Battle of Life.	Boswell and Johnson.
	History of the Free-Trade Movement in England.

Poultry Keeper, The Practical. By LEWIS WRIGHT. With Coloured Plates and Illustrations. 3s. 6d.

Poultry, The Book of. By LEWIS WRIGHT. *Popular Edition.* With Illustrations on Wood, 10s. 6d.

Poultry, The Illustrated Book of. By LEWIS WRIGHT. With Fifty Exquisite Coloured Plates, and numerous Wood Engravings. Cloth, 31s. 6d. ; half-morocco, £2 2s.

Printing Machinery and Letterpress Printing, Modern. By FRED. J. F. WILSON and DOUGLAS GREY. Illustrated. 21s.

Queen Victoria, The Life and Times of. By ROBERT WILSON. Complete in 2 Vols. With numerous Illustrations. 9s. each.

Queer Race, A. By W. WESTALL. Cloth, 5s.

Rabbit-Keeper, The Practical. By CUNICULUS. Illustrated. 3s. 6d.

Railway Library, Cassell's. Crown 8vo, boards, 2s. each.

Dead Man's Rock. By Q.	The Tragedy of Brinkwater. By Martha L. Moodey.
A Queer Race. By W. Westall.	An American Penman. By Julian Hawthorne.
Captain Trafalgar. By Westall and Laurie.	Section 558 ; or, The Fatal Letter. By Julian Hawthorne.
The Phantom City. By W. Westall.	The Brown Stone Boy. By W. H. Bishop.
Another's Crime. By Julian Hawthorne.	A Tragic Mystery. By Julian Hawthorne.
The Yoke of the Thorah. By Sidney Luska.	The Great Bank Robbery. By Julian Hawthorne.
Who is John Noman? By Charles Henry Beckett.	

Red Library of English and American Classics, The. Stiff covers, 1s. each ; cloth, 2s. each.

The Prairie.	Uncle Tom's Cabin.
Dombey and Son. Two Vols.	Deerslayer.
Night and Morning.	Eugene Aram.
Kenilworth.	Jack Hinton, the Guardsman.
The Ingoldsby Legends.	Rome and the Early Christians.
Tower of London.	The Trials of Margaret Lyndsay.
The Pioneers.	Edgar Allan Poe. Prose and Poetry, Selections from.
Charles O'Malley.	Old Mortality.
Barnaby Rudge.	The Hour and the Man.
Cakes and Ale.	Washington Irving's Sketch-Book.
The King's Own.	Last Days of Palmyra.
People I have Met.	Tales of the Borders.
The Pathfinder.	Pride and Prejudice.
Evelina.	Last of the Mohicans.
Scott's Poems.	Heart of Midlothian.
Last of the Barons.	Last Days of Pompeii.
Adventures of Mr. Ledbury.	Yellowplush Papers.
Ivanhoe.	Handy Andy.
Oliver Twist.	Selected Plays.
Selections from Hood's Works.	American Humour.
Longfellow's Prose Works.	Sketches by Boz.
Sense and Sensibility.	Macaulay's Lays and Selected Essays.
Lytton's Plays.	Harry Lorrequer.
Tales, Poems, and Sketches (Bret Harte).	Old Curiosity Shop.
Martin Chuzzlewit. Two Vols.	Rienzi.
The Prince of the House of David.	The Talisman.
Sheridan's Plays.	Pickwick. Two Vols.
	Scarlet Letter.

Rivers of Great Britain, The: Descriptive, Historical, Pictorial. RIVERS of THE EAST COAST. With numerous highly-finished Engravings. Royal 4to, with Etching as Frontispiece, 42s.

Rossetti, Dante Gabriel, as Designer and Writer. Notes by WILLIAM MICHAEL ROSSETTI. 7s. 6d.

Royal River, The: The Thames, from Source to Sea. With Descriptive Text and a Series of beautiful Engravings. £2 2s.

Russia. By Sir DONALD MACKENZIE WALLACE, M.A. 5s.

Russia, Truth about. By W. T. STEAD. Demy 8vo, cloth, 10s. 6d.

Russo-Turkish War, Cassell's History of. With about 500 Illustrations. Two Vols., 9s. each; library binding, One Vol., 15s.

St. Cuthbert's Tower. By FLORENCE WARDEN. Three Vols., cloth, 31s. 6d.

Saturday Journal, Cassell's. Yearly Vols., 7s. 6d.

Science for All. Edited by Dr. ROBERT BROWN, M.A., F.L.S., &c. *Revised Edition.* With 1,500 Illustrations. Five Vols., 9s. each.

Sea, The: Its Stirring Story of Adventure, Peril, and Heroism. By F. WHYMPER. With 400 Illustrations. Four Vols., 7s. 6d. each.

Secret of the Lamas, The. A Tale of Thibet. Crown 8vo, 5s.

Sent Back by the Angels; and other Ballads of Home and Homely Life. By FREDERICK LANGBRIDGE, M.A. *Popular Edition.* 1s.

Shaftesbury, The Seventh Earl of, K.G., The Life and Work of. By EDWIN HODDER. With Portraits. Three Vols., 36s. *Popular Edition,* in One Vol., 7s. 6d.

Shakspere, The International. *Édition de luxe.*
"King Henry IV." Illustrated by Herr EDUARD GRÜTZNER. £3 10s.
"As You Like It." Illustrated by Mons. EMILE BAYARD. £3 10s.
"Romeo and Juliet." Illustrated by FRANK DICKSEE, A.R.A. £5 5s.

Shakspere, The Leopold. With 400 Illustrations, and an Introduction by F. J. FURNIVALL. *Cheap Edition,* 3s. 6d. Small 4to, cloth gilt, gilt edges, 6s.; roxburgh, 7s. 6d.

Shakspere, The Royal. With Exquisite Steel Plates and Wood Engravings. Three Vols. 15s. each.

Shakespeare, Cassell's Quarto Edition. Edited by CHARLES and MARY COWDEN CLARKE, and containing about 600 Illustrations by H. C. SELOUS. Complete in Three Vols., cloth gilt, £3 3s.—Also published in Three separate Volumes, in cloth, viz.:—The COMEDIES, 21s.; The HISTORICAL PLAYS, 18s. 6d.; The TRAGEDIES, 25s.

Shakespeare, Miniature. Illustrated. In Twelve Vols., in box, 12s.; or in Red Paste Grain (box to match), with spring catch, lettered in gold, 21s.

Shakespeare, The England of. By E. GOADBY. Illustrated. *New Edition.* 2s. 6d.

Shakespearean Scenes and Characters. By AUSTIN BRERETON. Royal 4to, 21s.

Sketching from Nature in Water Colours. By AARON PENLEY. 15s.

Skin and Hair, The Management of the. By MALCOLM MORRIS, F.R.C.S. 2s.

Social Welfare, Subjects of. By the Rt. Hon. SIR LYON PLAYFAIR, M.P. 7s. 6d.

South Eastern Railway, The Official Illustrated Guide to The. 1s.; cloth, 2s.

Spectacles, How to Select, in Cases of Long, Short, and Weak Sight. By CHARLES BELL TAYLOR, F.R.C.S. and M.D., Edin. 1s.

Splendid Spur, The. Being Memories of the Adventures of Mr. JOHN MARVEL, a Servant of His late Majesty, King Charles I., in the years 1642-3. Written by himself. Edited in Modern English by "Q." Author of "Dead Man's Rock," &c. Crown 8vo, 5s.

Sports and Pastimes, Cassell's Complete Book of. *Cheap Edition.* With more than 900 Illustrations. Cloth, 3s. 6d.

Starland. Being Talks with Young People about the Wonders of the Heavens. By Sir ROBERT STAWELL BALL, LL.D., F.R.S., F.R.A.S. Illustrated. Crown 8vo, 6s.

Stock Exchange Year-Book, The. By THOMAS SKINNER. 12s. 6d.

Sunlight and Shade. With numerous Exquisite Engravings. 7s. 6d.

Thackeray, Character Sketches from. Six New and Original Drawings by FREDERICK BARNARD, reproduced in Photogravure. 21s.

Three and Sixpenny Library of Standard Tales, &c. All Illustrated and bound in cloth gilt. Crown 8vo. 3s. 6d. each.

Jane Austen and her Works.	The Half Sisters.
Mission Life in Greece and Palestine.	Peggy Oglivie's Inheritance.
The Romance of Trade.	The Family Honour.
The Three Homes.	Esther West.
Deepdale Vicarage.	Working to Win.
In Duty Bound.	Krilof and his Fables.

Fairy Tales. By Prof. Morley.

Tot Book for all Public Examinations. By W. S. THOMSON, M.A. 1s.

Treasure Island. By R. L. STEVENSON. Illustrated. 5s.

Treatment, The Year-Book of. A Critical Review for Practitioners of Medicine and Surgery. 5s.

Tree Painting in Water Colours. By W. H. J. BOOT. With Eighteen Coloured Plates, and valuable instructions by the Artist. 5s.

Trees, Familiar. By G. S. BOULGER, F.L.S., F.G.S. Two Series. With Forty full-page Coloured Plates by W. H. J. BOOT. 12s. 6d. each.

Triumphs of Engineering. With Eight full-page Illustrations. 5s.

Troy Town, The Astonishing History of. By Q., Author of "Dead Man's Rock." Crown 8vo, cloth, 5s.

Under a Strange Mask. By FRANK BARRETT. Illustrated. Two Vols. 12s.

"Unicode": The Universal Telegraphic Phrase Book. Pocket and Desk Editions. 2s. 6d. each.

United States, Cassell's History of the. By the late EDMUND OLLIER. With 600 Illustrations. Three Vols. 9s. each.

United States, The Youth's History of. By EDWARD S. ELLIS. Illustrated. Four Vols. 36s.

Universal History, Cassell's Illustrated. With nearly ONE THOUSAND ILLUSTRATIONS. Vol. I. Early and Greek History.—Vol. II. The Roman Period.—Vol. III. The Middle Ages.—Vol. IV. Modern History. 9s. each.

Vaccination Vindicated. An Answer to the leading Anti-Vaccinators. By JOHN C. McVAIL, M.D., D.P.H. Camb. 5s.

Veiled Beyond, The. A Novel. By S. B. ALEXANDER. Cloth, 3s. 6d.

Vicar of Wakefield and other Works by OLIVER GOLDSMITH. Illustrated. 3s. 6d.; cloth, gilt edges, 5s.

Water-Colour Painting, A Course of. With Twenty-four Coloured Plates by R. P. LEITCH, and full Instructions to the Pupil. 5s.

What Girls Can Do. By PHYLLIS BROWNE. 2s. 6d.

Wild Birds, Familiar. By W. SWAYSLAND. Four Series. With 40 Coloured Plates in each. 12s. 6d. each.

Wild Flowers, Familiar. By F. E. HULME, F.L.S., F.S.A. Five Series. With 40 Coloured Plates in each. 12s. 6d. each.

Wise Woman, The. By GEORGE MACDONALD. 2s. 6d.

Woman's World, The. Yearly Volume. 18s.

Wordsworth's Ode on Immortality, and Lines on Tintern Abbey. Fully Illustrated. Cloth, 2s. 6d.

World of Wit and Humour, The. With 400 Illustrations. Cloth, 7s. 6d.; cloth gilt, gilt edges, 10s. 6d.

World of Wonders, The. With 400 Illustrations. Two Vols. 7s. 6d. each.

World's Lumber Room, The. By SELINA GAYE. Illustrated. 2s. 6d.

Yule Tide. CASSELL'S CHRISTMAS ANNUAL. 1s.

ILLUSTRATED MAGAZINES.

The Quiver, for **Sunday and General Reading.** Monthly, 6d.

Cassell's Family Magazine. Monthly, 7d.

"Little Folks" Magazine. Monthly, 6d.

The Magazine of Art. Monthly, 1s.

The Woman's World. Monthly, 1s.

Cassell's Saturday Journal. Weekly, 1d.; Monthly, 6d.

Work. An Illustrated Magazine of Practice and Theory for all Workmen, Professional and Amateur. Weekly, 1d.; Monthly, 6d.

** *Full particulars of* CASSELL & COMPANY'S **Monthly Serial Publications** *will be found in* CASSELL & COMPANY'S COMPLETE CATALOGUE.

Catalogues of CASSELL & COMPANY'S PUBLICATIONS, which may be had at all Booksellers', or will be sent post free on application to the Publishers:—

CASSELL'S COMPLETE CATALOGUE, containing particulars of One Thousand Volumes.

CASSELL'S CLASSIFIED CATALOGUE, in which their Works are arranged according to price, from *Threepence to Fifty Guineas.*

CASSELL'S EDUCATIONAL CATALOGUE, containing particulars of CASSELL & COMPANY'S Educational Works and Students' Manuals.

CASSELL & COMPANY, LIMITED, *Ludgate Hill, London.*

Bibles and Religious Works.

Bible, Cassell's Illustrated Family. With 900 Illustrations. Leather, gilt edges, £2 10s. ; full morocco, £3 10s.

Bible Dictionary, Cassell's. With nearly 600 Illustrations. 7s. 6d. ; roxburgh, 10s. 6d.

Bible Educator, The. Edited by the Very Rev. Dean PLUMPTRE, D.D. With Illustrations, Maps, &c. Four Vols., cloth, 6s. each.

Bible Talks about Bible Pictures. Illustrated by GUSTAVE DORÉ and others. Large 4to, 5s.

Biblewomen and Nurses. Yearly Volume, 3s.

Bunyan's Pilgrim's Progress (Cassell's Illustrated). 4to. 7s. 6d.

Bunyan's Pilgrim's Progress. With Illustrations. *Popular Edition*, 3s. 6d.

Child's Bible, The. With 200 Illustrations. Demy 4to, 830 pp. 150th *Thousand*. *Cheap Edition*, 7s. 6d. *Superior Edition*, with 6 Coloured Plates, gilt edges, 10s. 6d.

Child's Life of Christ, The. Complete in One Handsome Volume, with about 200 Original Illustrations. *Cheap Edition*, cloth, 7s. 6d. ; or with 6 Coloured Plates, cloth, gilt edges, 10s. 6d. Demy 4to. gilt edges, 21s.

"Come, ye Children." By Rev. BENJAMIN WAUGH. Illustrated. 5s.

Commentary, The New Testament, for English Readers. Edited by the Rt. Rev. C. J. ELLICOTT, D.D., Lord Bishop of Gloucester and Bristol. In Three Volumes, 21s. each.

    Vol. I.—The Four Gospels.
    Vol. II.—The Acts, Romans, Corinthians, Galatians.
    Vol. III.—The remaining Books of the New Testament.

Commentary, The Old Testament, for English Readers. Edited by the Rt. Rev. C. J. ELLICOTT, D.D., Lord Bishop of Gloucester and Bristol. Complete in 5 Vols., 21s. each.

Vol. I.—Genesis to Numbers.	Vol. III.—Kings I. to Esther.
Vol. II.—Deuteronomy to Samuel II.	Vol. IV.—Job to Isaiah.
Vol. V.—Jeremiah to Malachi.	

Dictionary of Religion, The. An Encyclopædia of Christian and other Religious Doctrines, Denominations, Sects, Heresies, Ecclesiastical Terms, History, Biography, &c. &c. By the Rev. WILLIAM BENHAM, B.D. Cloth, 21s. ; roxburgh, 25s.

Doré Bible. With 230 Illustrations by GUSTAVE DORÉ. *Original Edition*. Two Vols., cloth, £8 ; best morocco, gilt edges, £15.

Early Days of Christianity, The. By the Ven. Archdeacon FARRAR, D.D., F.R.S.
    LIBRARY EDITION. Two Vols., 24s. ; morocco, £2 2s.
    POPULAR EDITION. Complete in One Volume, cloth, 6s. ; cloth, gilt edges, 7s. 6d. ; Persian morocco, 10s. 6d. ; tree-calf, 15s.

Family Prayer-Book, The. Edited by Rev. Canon GARBETT, M.A., and Rev. S. MARTIN. Extra crown 4to, cloth, 5s. ; morocco, 18s.

Geikie, Cunningham, D.D., Works by :—
    The Holy Land and the Bible. A Book of Scripture Illustrations gathered in Palestine. With Map. Two Vols., 24s.
    Hours with the Bible. Six Vols. 6s. each.
    Entering on Life. 3s. 6d.
    The Precious Promises. 2s. 6d.
    The English Reformation. 5s.
    Old Testament Characters. 6s.
    The Life and Words of Christ. Illustrated. Two Vols., cloth, 30s. *Library Edition*. Two Vols., cloth, 30s. *Students' Edition*, Two Vols., 16s. *Cheap Edition*, in One Vol. 7s. 6d.

Glories of the Man of Sorrows, The. Sermons preached at St. James's, Piccadilly. By the Rev. H. G. BONAVIA HUNT, Mus.D., F.R.S.Edin. 2s. 6d.

Gospel of Grace, The. By a LINDESIE. Cloth, 2s. 6d.

Helps to Belief. A Series of Helpful Manuals on the Religious Difficulties of the Day. Edited by the Rev. TEIGNMOUTH SHORE, M.A., Chaplain in Ordinary to the Queen. Cloth, 1s. each.

CREATION. By the Lord Bishop of Carlisle.	THE MORALITY OF THE OLD TESTAMENT. By the Rev. Newman Smyth, D.D.
MIRACLES. By the Rev. Brownlow Maitland, M.A.	
PRAYER. By the Rev. T. Teignmouth Shore, M.A.	THE DIVINITY OF OUR LORD. By the Lord Bishop of Derry.

    THE ATONEMENT. By the Lord Bishop of Peterborough.

"Heart Chords." A Series of Works by Eminent Divines. Bound in cloth, red ; edges, 1s. each.

My Father. By the Right Rev. Ashton Oxenden, late Bishop of Montreal.

My Bible. By the Rt. Rev. W. Boyd Carpenter, Bishop of Ripon.

My Work for God. By the Right Rev. Bishop Cotterill.

My Object in Life. By the Ven. Archdeacon Farrar, D.D.

My Aspirations. By the Rev. G. Matheson, D.D.

My Emotional Life. By the Rev. Preb. Chadwick, D.D.

My Body. By the Rev. Prof. W. G. Blaikie, D.D.

My Soul. By the Rev. P. B. Power, M.A.

My Growth in Divine Life. By the Rev. Prebendary Reynolds, M.A.

My Hereafter. By the Very Rev. Dean Bickersteth.

My Walk with God. By the Very Rev. Dean Montgomery.

My Aids to the Divine Life. By the Very Rev. Dean Boyle.

My Sources of Strength. By the Rev. E. E. Jenkins, M.A., Secretary of the Wesleyan Missionary Society.

Holy Land and the Bible, The. A Book of Scripture Illustrations gathered in Palestine. By the Rev. Cunningham Geikie, D.D. Two Vols., demy 8vo, 1,120 pages, with Map. Price 24s.

"I Must." Short Missionary Bible Readings. By Sophia M. Nugent. Enamelled cover, 6d. ; cloth, gilt edges, 1s.

Life of Christ, The. By the Ven. Archdeacon Farrar, D.D., F.R.S., Chaplain in Ordinary to the Queen.

Illustrated Edition, with about 300 Original Illustrations. Extra crown 4to, cloth, gilt edges, 21s. ; morocco antique, 42s.

Library Edition. Two Vols. Cloth, 24s. ; morocco, 42s.

Popular Edition, in One Vol. 8vo, cloth, 6s.; cloth, gilt edges, 7s. 6d. ; Persian morocco, gilt edges, 10s. 6d. ; tree-calf, 15s.

Marriage Ring, The. By William Landels, D.D. Bound in white leatherette, gilt edges, in box, 6s. ; French morocco, 8s. 6d.

Moses and Geology; or, the Harmony of the Bible with Science. By the Rev. Samuel Kinns, Ph.D., F.R.A.S. Illustrated. *Cheap Edition.* 6s.

Protestantism, The History of. By the Rev. J. A. Wylie, LL.D. Containing upwards of 600 Original Illustrations. Three Vols., 27s. ; Library Edition, 30s.

"Quiver" Yearly Volume, The. With about 600 Original Illustrations and Coloured Frontispiece. 7s. 6d. Also Monthly, 6d.

St. George for England; and other Sermons preached to Children. *Fifth Edition.* By the Rev. T. Teignmouth Shore, M.A. 5s.

St. Paul, The Life and Work of. By the Ven. Archdeacon Farrar, D.D., F.R.S., Chaplain in Ordinary to the Queen.

Library Edition. Two Vols., cloth, 24s. ; calf, 42s.

Illustrated Edition, complete in One Volume, with about 300 Illustrations, £1 1s. ; morocco, £2 2s.

Popular Edition. One Volume, 8vo, cloth, 6s. ; cloth, gilt edges, 7s. 6d. ; Persian morocco, 10s. 6d. ; tree-calf, 15s.

Secular Life, The Gospel of the. Sermons preached at Oxford. By the Hon. W. H. Fremantle, Canon of Canterbury. *Cheap Edition.* 2s. 6d.

Shall We Know One Another ? By the Rt. Rev. J. C. Ryle, D.D., Bishop of Liverpool. *New and Enlarged Edition.* Cloth limp, 1s.

Stromata. By the Ven. Archdeacon Sheringham, M.A. 2s. 6d.

"Sunday." Its Origin, History, and Present Obligation. By the Ven. Archdeacon Hessey, D.C.L. *Fifth Edition.* 7s. 6d.

Twilight of Life, The: Words of Counsel and Comfort for the Aged. By John Ellerton, M.A. 1s. 6d.

Voice of Time, The. By John Stroud. Cloth gilt, 1s.

Educational Works and Students' Manuals.

Alphabet, Cassell's Pictorial. Size, 35 inches by 42½ inches. Mounted on Linen, with rollers. 3s. 6d.

Arithmetics, The Modern School. By GEORGE RICKS, B.Sc. Lond. With Test Cards. (*List on application.*)

Book-Keeping. By THEODORE JONES. FOR SCHOOLS, 2s. ; or cloth, 3s. FOR THE MILLION, 2s. ; or cloth, 3s. Books for Jones's System, Ruled Sets of, 2s.

Chemistry, The Public School. By J. H. ANDERSON, M.A. 2s. 6d.

Commentary, The New Testament. Edited by Bishop ELLICOTT. Handy Volume Edition. Suitable for School and general use.

St. Matthew. 3s. 6d.	Romans. 2s. 6d.	Titus, Philemon, Hebrews, and James. 3s.
St. Mark. 3s.	Corinthians I and II. 3s.	Peter, Jude, and John. 3s.
St. Luke. 3s. 6d.	Galatians, Ephesians, and Philippians. 3s.	The Revelation. 3s.
St. John. 3s. 6d.	Colossians, Thessalonians, and Timothy. 3s.	An Introduction to the New Testament. 2s. 6d.
The Acts of the Apostles. 3s. 6d.		

Commentary, The Old Testament. Edited by Bishop ELLICOTT. Handy Volume Edition. Suitable for School and general use.

Genesis. 3s. 6d.	Leviticus. 3s.	Deuteronomy. 2s. 6d.
Exodus. 3s.	Numbers. 2s. 6d.	

Copy-Books, Cassell's Graduated. Complete in 18 Books. 2d. each.

Copy-Books, The Modern School. Complete in 12 Books. 2d. each.

Drawing Copies, Cassell's "New Standard." Fourteen Books :—

Books A to F, for Standards I. to IV.	.. .. ..	2d. each.
" G, H, K, L, M, O, for Standards V. to VII.	:: :: ..	3d. each.
" N, P, ...	:: :: ..	4d. each.

Drawing Copies, Cassell's Modern School Freehand. First Grade, 1s. ; Second Grade, 2s.

Electricity, Practical. By Prof. W. E. AYRTON. 7s. 6d.

Energy and Motion: A Text-Book of Elementary Mechanics. By WILLIAM PAICE, M.A. Illustrated. 1s. 6d.

English Literature, A First Sketch of, from the Earliest Period to the Present Time. By Prof. HENRY MORLEY. 7s. 6d.

Euclid, Cassell's. Edited by Prof. WALLACE, M.A. 1s.

Euclid, The First Four Books of. In paper, 6d. ; cloth, 9d.

French, Cassell's Lessons in. *New and Revised Edition.* Parts I. and II., each 2s. 6d. ; complete, 4s. 6d. Key, 1s. 6d.

French-English and English-French Dictionary. *Entirely New and Enlarged Edition.* 1,150 pages, 8vo, cloth, 3s. 6d.

French Reader, Cassell's Public School. By GUILLAUME S. CONRAD. 2s. 6d.

Galbraith and Haughton's Scientific Manuals. By the Rev. Prof. GALBRAITH, M.A., and the Rev. Prof. HAUGHTON, M.D., D.C.L.

Plane Trigonometry. 2s. 6d.	Optics. 2s. 6d.
Euclid. Books I., II., III. 2s. 6d. Books IV., V., VI. 2s. 6d.	Hydrostatics. 3s. 6d.
Mathematical Tables. 3s. 6d.	Astronomy. 5s.
Mechanics. 3s. 6d.	Steam Engine. 3s. 6d.
Natural Philosophy. 3s. 6d.	Algebra. Part I., cloth, 2s. 6d. Complete, 7s. 6d. Tides and Tidal Currents, with Tidal Cards, 3s.

Geometry, First Elements of Experimental. By PAUL BERT. Fully Illustrated. 1s. 6d.

Geometry, Practical Solid. By Major ROSS, R.E. 2s.

German Dictionary, Cassell's New. German-English, English-German. Cloth, 7s. 6d. ; half-morocco, 9s.

German of To-Day. By Dr. HEINEMANN. 1s. 6d.

German Reading, First Lessons in. By A. JAGST. Illustrated. 1s.

Hand and Eye Training. By G. RICKS, B.Sc. Two Vols., with 16 Coloured Plates in each Vol. Crown 4to, 6s. each.

Handbook of New Code of Regulations. By JOHN F. MOSS. *New and Revised Edition.* 1s. ; cloth, 2s.

Historical Cartoons, Cassell's Coloured. Size 45 in. × 35 in. 2s. each. Mounted on canvas and varnished, with rollers, 5s. each. (Descriptive pamphlet, 16 pp., 1d.)

Historical Course for Schools, Cassell's. Illustrated throughout. I.—Stories from English History, 1s. II.—The Simple Outline of English History, 1s. 3d. III.—The Class History of England, 2s. 6d.

Latin-English Dictionary, Cassell's. Thoroughly revised and corrected, and in part re-written by J. R. V. MARCHANT, M.A. 3s. 6d.

Latin-English and English-Latin Dictionary. By J. R. BEARD, D.D., and C. BEARD, B.A. Crown 8vo, 914 pp., 3s. 6d.

Latin Primer, The New. By Prof. J. P. POSTGATE. 2s. 6d.

Laws of Every-Day Life. For the Use of Schools. By H. O. ARNOLD-FORSTER. 1s. 6d. *Presentation Edition*, 3s. 6d.

Lay Texts for the Young, in English and French. By Mrs. RICHARD STRACHEY. 2s. 6d.

Little Folks' History of England. By ISA CRAIG-KNOX. Illustrated. 1s. 6d.

Making of the Home, The : A Book of Domestic Economy for School and Home Use. By Mrs. SAMUEL A. BARNETT. 1s. 6d.

Marlborough Books :—

Arithmetic Examples. 3s.	French Exercises. 3s. 6d.
Arithmetic Rules. 1s. 6d.	French Grammar. 2s. 6d.

German Grammar. 3s. 6d.

Mechanics and Machine Design, Numerical Examples in Practical. By R. G. BLAINE, M.E. With Diagrams. Cloth, 2s. 6d.

"Model Joint" Wall Sheets, for Instruction in Manual Training. By S. BARTER. Eight Sheets, 2s. 6d. each.

Music, An Elementary Manual of. By HENRY LESLIE. 1s.

Popular Educator, Cassell's New. With Revised Text, New Maps, New Coloured Plates, New Type, &c. To be completed in Eight Vols., 5s. each.

Popular Educator, Cassell's. Complete in SIX Vols., 5s. each.

Reader, The Citizen. By H. O. ARNOLD-FORSTER. 1s. 6d.

Reader, The Temperance. By Rev. J. DENNIS HIRD. Crown 8vo, 1s. 6d.

Readers, Cassell's "Higher Class" :— "The World's Lumber Room," Illustrated, 2s. 6d.; "Short Studies from Nature," Illustrated, 2s. 6d.; "The World in Pictures." (Ten in Series.) Cloth, 2s. each. (*List on application.*)

Readers, Cassell's Historical. Illustrated throughout, printed on superior paper, and strongly bound in cloth. (*List on application.*)

Readers, Cassell's Readable. Carefully graduated, extremely interesting, and Illustrated throughout. (*List on application*)

Readers for Infant Schools, Coloured. Three Books. Each containing 48 pages, including 8 pages in colours. 4d. each.

Readers, The Modern Geographical. Illustrated throughout. (*List on application.*)

Readers, The Modern School. Illustrated. (*List on application.*)

Reading and Spelling Book, Cassell's Illustrated. 1s.

School Bank Manual, A. By AGNES LAMBERT. 6d.

Sculpture, A Primer of. By E. ROSCOE MULLINS. Illustrated. 2s. 6d.

Shakspere Reading Book, The. By H. COURTHOPE BOWEN, M.A. Illustrated. 3s. 6d. Also issued in Three Books, 1s. each.

Shakspere's Plays for School Use. Illustrated. 5 Books. 6d. each.

Spelling, A Complete Manual of. By J. D. MORELL, LL.D. 1s.

Technical Educator, Cassell's. Illustrated throughout. Four Vols., 5s. each.

Technical Manuals, Cassell's. Illustrated throughout.

Handrailing and Staircasing. 3s. 6d.	Machinists & Engineers, Drawing for. 4s.6d.
Bricklayers, Drawing for. 3s.	Model Drawing. 3s.
Building Construction. 2s.	Orthographical and Isometrical Projection. 2s.
Cabinet-Makers, Drawing for. 3s.	
Carpenters & Joiners, Drawing for. 3s. 6d.	Practical Perspective. 3s.
Gothic Stonework. 3s.	Stonemasons, Drawing for. 3s.
Linear Drawing & Practical Geometry. 2s.	Applied Mechanics. By Sir R. S. Ball, LL.D. 2s.
Linear Drawing and Projection. The Two Vols. in One, 3s. 6d.	Systematic Drawing and Shading. By Charles Ryan. 2s.
Metal-Plate Workers, Drawing for. 3s.	

Technology, Manuals of. Edited by Prof. AYRTON, F.R.S., and RICHARD WORMELL, D.Sc., M.A. Illustrated throughout.

The Dyeing of Textile Fabrics. By Prof. Hummel. 5s.	Design in Textile Fabrics. By T. R. Ashenhurst. 4s. 6d.
Watch and Clock Making. By D. Glasgow, Vice-President of the British Horological Institute. 4s. 6d.	Spinning Woollen and Worsted. By W. S. McLaren, M.P. 4s .6d.
	Practical Mechanics. By Prof. Perry, M.E. 3s. 6d.
Steel and Iron. By Prof. W. H. Greenwood, F.C.S., M.I.C.E., &c. 5s.	Cutting Tools Worked by Hand and Machine. By Prof. Smith. 3s 6d.

Test Cards, Cassell's Combination. In sets, 1s. each.

Test Cards, Cassell's Modern School. In sets, 1s. each.

A Copy of Cassell and Company's Complete Catalogue will be forwarded post free on application.

Books for Young People.

"Little Folks" Half-Yearly Volume. Containing 432 pages of Letterpress, with Pictures on nearly every page, together with Two Full-page Plates printed in Colours and Four Tinted Plates. Coloured boards, 3s. 6d. ; or cloth gilt, gilt edges, 5s.

Bo-Peep. A Book for the Little Ones. With Original Stories and Verses. Illustrated with beautiful Pictures on nearly every page. Yearly Volume. Elegant picture boards, 2s. 6d. ; cloth gilt, gilt edges, 3s. 6d.

Cassell's Pictorial Scrap Book, containing nearly two thousand Pictures beautifully printed and handsomely bound in one large volume. Coloured boards, 15s. ; cloth lettered, 21s.

Legends for Lionel. New Picture Book by WALTER CRANE. 5s.

Flora's Feast. A Masque of Flowers. Penned and Pictured by WALTER CRANE. With 40 pages in Colours. 5s.

The New Children's Album. Fcap. 4to, 320 pages. Illustrated throughout. 3s. 6d.

The Tales of the Sixty Mandarins. By P. V. RAMASWAMI RAJU. 5s.

Gift Books for Young People. By Popular Authors. With Four Original Illustrations in each. Cloth gilt, 1s. 6d. each.

The Boy Hunters of Kentucky. By Edward S. Ellis.	Frank's Life-Battle.
Red Feather: a Tale of the American Frontier. By Edward S. Ellis.	Major Monk's Motto; or, "Look Before you Leap."
Fritters; or, "It's a Long Lane that has no Turning."	Tim Thomson's Trial; or, "All is not Gold that Glitters."
Trixy; or, "Those who Live in Glass Houses shouldn't throw Stones."	Ursula's Stumbling-Block.
The Two Hardcastles.	Ruth's Life-Work; or, "No Pains, no Gains."
Seeking a City.	Rags and Rainbows.
Rhoda's Reward.	Uncle William's Charge.
Jack Marston's Anchor.	Pretty Pink's Purpose.

Books for Young People. Price 2s. 6d. each.

Heroes of Every-day Life. By Laura Lane. Illustrated.	Early Explorers. By Thomas Frost.
Decisive Events in History. By Thomas Archer. With Original Illustrations.	Home Chat with our Young Folks. Illustrated throughout.
The True Robinson Crusoes.	Jungle, Peak, and Plain. Illustrated throughout.
Peeps Abroad for Folks at Home. Illustrated.	The World's Lumber Room. By Selina Gaye.

"Golden Mottoes" Series, The. Each Book containing 208 pages, with Four full-page Original Illustrations. Crown 8vo, cloth gilt, 2s. each.

"Nil Desperandum." By the Rev. F. Langbridge, M.A.	"Honour is my Guide." By Jeanie Hering (Mrs. Adams-Acton).
"Bear and Forbear." By Sarah Pitt.	"Aim at a Sure End." By Emily Searchfield.
"Foremost if I Can." By Helen Atteridge.	"He Conquers who Endures." By the Author of "May Cunningham's Trial," &c.

The "Cross and Crown" Series. Consisting of Stories founded on incidents which occurred during Religious Persecutions of Past Days. With Illustrations in each Book. 2s. 6d. each.

By Fire and Sword: a Story of the Huguenots. By Thomas Archer.	Strong to Suffer. By E. Wynne.
Adam Hepburn's Vow: a Tale of Kirk and Covenant. By Annie S. Swan.	Heroes of the Indian Empire; or, Stories of Valour and Victory. By Ernest Foster.
No. XIII.; or, The Story of the Lost Vestal. By Emma Marshall.	In Letters of Flame: A Story of the Waldenses. By C. L. Mateaux.
	Through Trial to Triumph. By Madeline B. Hunt.

The World's Workers. A Series of New and Original Volumes by Popular Authors. With Portraits printed on a tint as Frontispiece. 1s. each.

Dr. Arnold, of Rugby. By Rose E. Selfe.	Dr. Guthrie, Father Mathew, Elihu Burritt, Joseph Livesey.
The Earl of Shaftesbury.	Sir Henry Havelock and Colin Campbell, Lord Clyde.
Sarah Robinson, Agnes Weston, and Mrs. Meredith.	Abraham Lincoln.
Thomas A. Edison and Samuel F. B. Morse.	David Livingstone.
Mrs. Somerville and Mary Carpenter.	George Muller and Andrew Reed.
General Gordon.	Richard Cobden.
Charles Dickens.	Benjamin Franklin.
Sir Titus Salt and George Moore.	Handel.
Florence Nightingale, Catherine Marsh, Frances Ridley Havergal, Mrs. Ranyard ("L. N. R.").	Turner the Artist.
	George and Robert Stephenson.